"I thought Sparks would make a great running back...Derek has quickness and size. I hated to lose him."
— **JESSE CROW, FORMER HEAD COACH, WHARTON HIGH SCHOOL**

"I've been in education for 18 years, and I've never seen anything like it."
— **PAT MURPHY, PRINCIPAL, MATER DEI CATHOLIC HIGH SCHOOL**

"Sparks' career was a long, strange trip that left Sparks disillusioned. But he realizes it was a trip he had to take. As a result, Sparks blesses other student-athletes with his life story between the lines."
— **STEVE BERGUM, SPORTS WRITER**

"He's got eye-popping statistics, a quirky past and seemingly unlimited potential. But what's most impressive about Washington State University...football player, Derek Sparks, is his maturity. ...Sparks remains intent on his goals, while keeping things in perspective."
— **TIM SULLIVAN, SPORTS WRITER**

"He has impressed members of the California community with his maturity and strength of character...Despite all of the problems that Valley Prep and Derek have endured, everybody still likes Derek. It's not his fault at all. He's a popular, friendly kid."
— **JOHN LYNCH, SPORTS WRITER, *LOS ANGELES TIMES***

"His book, *Lessons of the Game*...validates his vision for a better student-athlete in society. Derek recognizes that life isn't a sport...He is a soldier for changing the ills in sport...I will be using this book for my Sports Management and Communication classes for years to come."
— **C.K. HARRISON, ED.D., DIRECTOR, THE PAUL ROBESON RESEARCH CENTER FOR ACADEMIC & ATHLETIC PROWESS, UNIVERSITY OF MICHIGAN**

"Derek Sparks had a reputation as a fast mover, on the field and between schools. He was as famous for his transfers as he was for his touchdowns."
— **ROB FERNAS, SPORTS WRITER, *LOS ANGELES TIMES***

"The first time Derek Sparks carried the ball for Mater Dei, he made a quick cut to the right then ran straight up the sideline for an 80-yard touchdown. It's not like Sparks to take such a direct route."
— **STEVE FRYER, *ORANGE COUNTY REGISTER***

"The Derek Sparks story, a book that others might benefit from...focuses on Derek's controversial athletic career...His tale involves under-the-table offers of cash and cars, grade-fixing and blackballing by spurned high schools, is common among highly prized young athletes."
  — **SHELDON SPENCER, SPORTS WRITER, *SEATTLE POST INTELLIGENCER***

"Derek Sparks has exposed the price of heroism as well as the price of ignorance. His exposé of the shame behind the scenes of student athletic programs is a primer for parents of young children and the answer for the parents of abandoned young athletes who wonder what went wrong?' This story would make an inspirational movie of the week."
  — **SUSAN NICKELLS, INDEPENDENT PRODUCER,**
    TELEVISION AND FILM

"This book should...serve as a warning to parents that not all teachers and coaches are looking out for the best interest of their children."
  — **VALERIE A. RICHARD, DIRECTOR OF CHAMPIONSHIPS,**
    WEST COAST CONFERENCE

"*Lessons of the Game* is one of the most in-depth, honest, and insightful autobiographies you will ever read. This is the story of a colorful, at times tragic, yet ultimately inspiring life that will leave you moved and cheering."
  — **ANTHONY McCLANAHAN, CALGARY STAMPEDERS,**
    CANADIAN FOOTBALL LEAGUE (CFL)

Sparks ..."*Lessons of the Game* is a must read for all potential athletes and their parents, but especially for African-American parents. The story of this young man's triumph over corruption, callousness and betrayal at such a young age is riveting. To come through with his mind and heart intact shows that athletes today need more than their God given talents if they are to stay healthy, rooted in moral values and sane."
  — **SANDRA CARTER, VICE PRESIDENT,**
    LOS ANGELES URBAN LEAGUE

"This is the most shocking story I have heard in my 20 years of association with athletics, you don't get this kind of stuff on the NCAA level."
  — **STAN THOMAS, FORMER COMMISSIONER OF ATHLETICS,**
    CALIFORNIA INTERSCHOLASTIC FEDERATION (CIF)

"Sparks has an amazing ability to remain focused...a trait that helped him endure an especially tumultuous football career."
— **CHRIS DESTEFANO, *SPORTS WASHINGTON MAGAZINE***

"Derek Sparks is a young man whose life has been mired in controversy...The door was open to confusion and corruption, something not unusual to...high school athletes..."
— **SHELLY SMITH, ESPN SPORTS REPORTER**

"Collectively there are millions of young men and women with ambitions to make it to some professional level of sports, they should know they have a better chance of winning the lottery than making a collegiate or professional roster."
— **Cornell Ward, Head Football Coach, Compton Community College**

"We, as coaches, must understand how much power we have when a child's dreams depend on us. We cannon mistreat or misuse the power that is given to us. We cannot break the rules. We cannot!"
— **Greg Burns, All-Pac-10 Conference Defensive Back, Assistant Coach, University of Louisville**

"*Lessons of the Game* should be required reading for all young people involved in athletics with hopes of a collegiate or professional sports career."
— **KENNY EASLEY, UCLA ALUMNI, Former Defensive Back, Seattle Seahawks**

"People have misjudged Derek. He got a bum rap from the media..."
— **Al "Buzz" Preston, Former Running Back Coach, Washington State University; Currently Offensive Coordinator, University of Nevada Las Vegas**

"Derek's life story is one of perseverance and determination. His story is a dramatic tale of resilience. It is indeed fascinating."
— **Dr. Renford Reese, Ph.D., University of Southern California**

"With his talents, Derek Sparks is a kid who could go on to Notre Dame or any Ivy League school. He is the type of kid we want to attend Mater Dei High School."
— **Lyle Porter, Former Principal, Mater Dei Catholic High School**

"...Derek is a productive young man who works hard at what he does and wants to succeed more than anything. I think he will."
— **TED WILLIAMS, ASSISTANT COACH, PHILADELPHIA EAGLES**

"He's worked through all types of adversity, and he just keeps coming back and coming back. He's used his experience to deliver something positive."
— **MIKE PRICE, HEAD FOOTBALL COACH, WASHINGTON STATE UNIVERSITY; 1998 COACH OF THE YEAR**

"Derek is on the right track in terms of the issues he is raising...With so few athletes today reaching the professional ranks, it is vital, if not critical, that we promote the advantages of a good education."
— **DEAN CROWLEY, COMMISSIONER OF ATHLETICS, (CIF) CALIFORNIA INTERSCHOLASTIC FEDERATION**

"What Derek demonstrated is a quiet confidence...To demonstrate that type of ability...is a tribute to his intestinal fortitude and his athletic ability. He's got strength, he's got speed...but I think his best quality is balance. He's very difficult to knock down. He's proven that his entire life."
— **BRUCE ROLLINSON, HEAD COACH, MATER DEI CATHOLIC HIGH SCHOOL**

"Derek's story is just one of millions [of] inner-city youth and sports...A real story behind the line."
— **ANGELO JACKSON, ASST. HEAD FOOTBALL COACH, COMPTON COLLEGE**

"Derek is a great kid...I think a lot of people...spoke out about Derek without knowing all the facts."
— **FATHER WELING, PRIEST MATER DEI CATHOLIC HIGH SCHOOL**

"*Lessons of the Game* is a must read for young athletes and their parents."
— **JEAN BOYD, CAREER DEVELOPMENT, ARIZONA STATE UNIVERSITY**

"He's not only the premier back in Southern California, but he's among the top 10 across the country."
— **DICK LASCOLA, HIGH SCHOOL RECRUITER**

LESSONS
OF THE
GAME

LESSONS OF THE GAME

Edited by
Valerie Shaw, M.PR

GAME TIME™
PUBLISHING

First published in the United States of American in 1999 by Derek Sparks
Cover design by Eric Mai illustration design.
Book layout and design by Dotti Albertine.

First draft edited by: Thomas Black
Edited by Valerie Shaw
10 9 8 7 6 5 4 3 2 1

Library of Congress Cataloging-in-Publication Data

Sparks, Derek

LESSONS OF THE GAME / by Derek Sparks with Stuart K Robinson
p. cm.
ISBN #0-9671471-1-5 : $19.95
1.Education. 2. The Game of life. 3. Students & Parents.
I. Sparks, Derek II. Title

LESSONS
OF THE
GAME

*The betrayal
of an All-American
football star*

BY
DEREK SPARKS
WITH
STUART K. ROBINSON

DEDICATION

This book, my autobiography,
is dedicated to my mother, June Sparks,
who loves and supports me unconditionally.

To Uncle Jerome and Aunt Gretta Sparks,
who gave me the opportunity to reach for the stars.
Much love!

In loving memory of teammates
Leon 'LB' Bender and Buddy Waldron.
Cougar legends live on!

In memory, too, of
Sarah Corson, a beloved friend.

CONTENTS

FOREWORD

Lessons of the Game is a candid portrayal of the pitfalls, expectations, and pressures today's high school athlete must endure. It is a journey created by high-stakes recruiting wars within both the high school and college ranks, in an arena where the only objective is to win.

This story brings to light the ulterior motives of many coaches, recruiters, administrators, and alumni. These are people of authority who will do anything to get an academically disadvantaged, but athletically talented youngster, into their high school or university.

Some of the things you'll read in this book might be shocking. They are, however, the true accounts of one of the most highly recruited student athletes in California High School sports history.

As Derek's agent, I am blessed with the opportunity to know this athletically gifted and driven young man. He tells this story in hopes of delivering a message too many fail to see: "Through education, we regain the advantage this system holds over us."

It is Derek's character that will allow him to succeed on and off the football field. With Derek's "football clock" ticking, it will not be an easy road. However, football is not everything to Derek, as it once was. It is still a passion, and it always will be. But if he makes it this time, it won't be for the fame or trappings of wealth. It will be for the great chance to show everyone how to really play..."THE GAME."

SEAN RICHMOND
PETER SPORTS MANAGEMENT
NAPA, CA

INTRODUCTION

As a kid, I never played football. The sandlots and the streets were my first fields. One of my earliest memories of football was watching the hard-hitting Oakland Raider, Lester Hayes. I saw him play in the Super Bowl and said to myself, "I'll be there one day."

On a Sunday, in January, 1992, as a member of the Dallas Cowboys, that day arrived. Super Bowl XXVII was held in Pasadena, Ca., the Rose Bowl. It was the same field I had played on during my collegiate days at UCLA, and it had one final memory to offer me. The one I had spent a lifetime dreaming of.

In January of 1993, I made a return visit to the Super Bowl, and with those two amazing experiences, I found my career surpassing my wildest fantasies. This game has brought me years of great memories, but many, over time, are blurred. I'm thankful for my career and my accomplishments, but there was a huge price to pay for the privilege of rising to the top.

Today, becoming a professional athlete is perhaps the most sought after career goal amongst our youth. Without knowing the tremendous odds (against them) or the price they must pay, their ultimate goal in life is to become superstars.

More often than not, parents, family, coaches, school administrators and alumni become influential in the development of that distant dream. With a "win at all costs" philosophy, they are unwitting partners in bending the rules of the game.

How often does a young athlete hear those closest to him say that grades don't matter or that it's okay to skip class? How often is that young athlete encouraged to perform with excellence on the field or the court; but not in the classroom?

Young athletes chasing the dream of sports stardom should realize that education is the dream they should be pursuing. It's a proven fact that the vast majority of student-athletes end their careers uneducated. In all too many cases, yesterday's high school, collegiate, and professional superstar becomes today's unskilled and under employed adult.

Beyond the competitive odds of stardom, the rigorous schedule, required discipline, and inevitable injuries make the dream transitory for all but a few athletes. A young aspiring football player should know that an average career in the NFL is a meager 4.7 years.

The reality is that millions of children who play sports never go on to play at the varsity high school or college levels, no less in the professional ranks. At whatever level, the student-athlete often finds him or herself facing unexpected pressures beyond the field of "play."

Read the tragic story of high school All-American football star Derek Sparks, who faced those pressures and was nearly destroyed by them. His courageous story of faith and perseverance against the "sports machine" is a valuable lesson for athletes and students of all ages.

Lessons of the Game will help young athletes, their parents and everyone who cares about their whole lives, not just their careers, to understand the real world of competitive sports. It is a vivid and telling illustration of how the system can be, and often is, unfair. But, through education, says Derek, in his inspirational autobiography, "The world is so very, very bright."

Derek is an inspired and motivated young man who has a three-fold purpose. Derek seeks to make a difference in the way we think of the student-athlete; and he hopes his message influences the way the student-athlete thinks of him or herself. Ultimately, Derek's message is offered to all of us in our quest to survive the real Lessons of the Game.

James Washington
Dallas Cowboys, 1990-1995

This story is true. It is not only true for me, but for more than a million other young men and women across America. The facts may shock you; but, believe it! I decided to change some of the names to shield the innocent, protecting them from the guilty. I have also changed the names of two of the schools. It was not, and is not my intent to seek revenge against any person or institution; I am simply answering my call. That call is to empower youth and parents with valuable information they may not be privy to elsewhere.

The reason this story may shock you is because few athletes, at any level, "talk" about their experiences. See, "talking" means breaking the rules; violating the unspoken code amongst athletes. Other athletes have done it — talked about what really goes on — but usually it is towards the end of their careers.

Putting my words on the pages of this book has allowed me to heal from my turbulent past as one of the most controversial high school football players to ever play the game. I pray that it is a healing not only for me, but for the sports society as a whole. I pray that my catharsis offers insight to other young athletes — men and women — who have faced or will face these same challenges.

1. EXILE

I should have let the phone ring. I knew better. All of my life I have trusted my instincts. I've learned to listen to the quiet voice deep inside of me, to let it guide me to the right decision. The telephone kept ringing. I knew better, but I picked it up anyway.

I was in the middle of packing my things, preparing to move on to what would be my fourth high school in four years. My career by this point had become as infamous for its controversy, as it had become famous for its accomplishments. "Touchdown" and "Scandal" had become prerequisite mentions to any news article about me.

This particular scandal started when I stepped off the airplane at LAX, returning from an invitational game in Hawaii. My two uncles, Jay and Tom met me at the plane. They had only one thing to say.

"Pack your stuff."

I had felt it coming, but I wasn't ready. Jay came to the point without ceremony. "It's over for the Prep, D."

I wanted to hit somebody. I wanted to cry. I wanted to scream. I wanted to be in control of my life.

The media had already had a field day painting me as this troubled athlete who couldn't stay at a school for more than a year. Now I was moving on again.

Besides the bad timing, I didn't feel right picking up and leaving my teammates who had become like family.

I would begin my senior year without a school, without a team. Just a horde of recruiters and media, wondering what the hell was up with that Sparks kid.

Now, I stood alone in my room, holding the phone in my hand, stunned, and turning over Jay's mandate in my head.

The voice on the other end wasted no time.

"I'll tell you what, kid," the voice said, "you'll never play organized football again. We'll see to that. You can kiss your senior year good-bye. And you can take all of those letters you got from colleges and shove them...

"As for your scholarship to USC or UCLA, you can flush that dream. We'll have that offer canceled before you can hang up the receiver!"

I knew that voice. I was once one of his blue-chip favorites.

"We made an investment in you, gave you the best of everything, and you had no problem with any of it.

"Did you think you could just spit in our faces now and walk away? Just watch how fast we take this away from you, you loser.

"This is your wake-up call!"

Click.

I stood there for a long time with the telephone receiver in my hand, cursing myself for ever picking it up, but it was a confrontation I couldn't have avoided. Although I was only a 16-year-old kid, and they were the adults who had been guiding my future, these guys wanted revenge.

To them, I had sold out in the worst possible way. I had crossed the line. As a student-athlete, I was expected to keep quiet, stay loyal, and just run the damn football.

Just run the football. Their motto rang in my head, as I stood there, dazed and shaking.

"Just run the football." Don't ask questions. Don't think. Don't hesitate. Just run the football.

If you had the gift, everything would be taken care of. *Everything.* School, family, friends, and finances. You name it.

I don't even think that it's ever explicitly said. You just know. Things will be taken care of. Do you have a problem with a certain subject in school? It's taken care of. Do you need new sneakers? Taken care of. A run-in with the law? Not a problem. That will be taken care of too.

I've never had any trouble with the law. I never intend to. But back then, I knew that if I ever did get in trouble with the police, it would somehow be taken care of. So long as, that is, I *just* ran the football.

I stood next to my single suitcase, containing everything I owned. Beside me was a box of college scholarship offers now worth no more than tickets to last year's Super Bowl game.

I was about to lose everything I had because I was not playing the game. Not their way, that is. I looked at the telephone in my hand, and for the first time in as long as I could remember, I began to cry.

2. ROOTS

Wharton, Texas. Don't feel bad if you've never heard of it. There's not much to Wharton, much less any reason you would be familiar with it.

People sometimes ask me what my hometown is known for. You know, like L.A. is known for show business, and New Orleans is known for its Mardi Gras? But Wharton? Honestly, I can't tell you what it's famous for; unless there's some notoriety that comes from putting a whole lot of poor people and drugs together in one place.

Even at that, there aren't that many people. Today Wharton's total population is approximately eight thousand. Wharton is located about fifty miles southwest of Houston. Beyond that, I guess the best thing I can say about it, is that I got out. Most of my relatives and friends are still there. Somehow they get by.

I was born when my mother was just 19-years-old. I'm an only child but that was all it took to prevent Mom from pursuing a real education so she could qualify for a decent job.

She and my father never married. He conveniently lost interest in her when she became pregnant with me. He was out of there before I took my first breath. So you can guess there wasn't a whole lot of money in our household while I was growing up.

Mom did the best she could and took whatever odd jobs she found. For a while she worked on a small factory assembly line. She was caught in a continuous cycle of layoffs and unemployment.

Fortunately, we had a huge close-knit family and when times got tough everyone pitched in. That seemed to be tradition for families in Wharton.

For years it didn't bother me not having a father in our house. That was the way it had always been. It wasn't until I was old enough to start hanging around other kids that it even occurred to me there was *supposed* to be a man in every household. My mother never talked about my father, or even hinted that I had one, so I never gave it much thought until I got a little older.

I didn't know it at the time, but my mom was in a state of depression that began with my birth. Even today, I can only imagine how hard it must have been for her. How different her life must have turned out from her early dreams.

With my birth, life had taken a hard turn for Mom. But she never let it show and she never gave up. She was always there for me, putting me first, raising me to be a good person. A responsible person. She viewed her situation as an opportunity to salvage something. To create something good. I hope she's pleased with the results.

When I was 12-years-old we moved to the projects, one of those government housing deals where the amount of rent you pay is based on your income.

My mom was often without a job, which meant that we were frequently on County Assistance. Food stamps, government cheese and rent subsidy. Sometimes our rent was fifteen dollars a month. This hardly raised an eyebrow in Wharton. Almost everybody was poor.

It wasn't until I started playing sports that I began to notice my teammates being dropped off and picked up by their fathers. Fathers were people who practiced ball with their sons. Men who told them stories. Taught them how to be responsible men.

I asked Mom about fathers. My father. But what could she say to make me feel better? I could tell that my questions hurt her as much as they did me. She didn't have any answers. How could she? Sometimes, age has nothing to do with understanding things. It hurt me to ask about my father and it hurt her not to answer.

My main male role model and father figure was my Uncle Jay. I wanted to be like Jay. I wanted to impress him. I wanted him to notice me. Jay had been a high school baseball star, so I pictured myself becoming a baseball player just like Jay.

That all changed one Sunday. I was 10-years-old. Jay, who was visiting from California, and a bunch of other family members, were watching a football game at Big Mamma's house.

Everybody was yelling and cheering, exchanging high-fives and performing their own rendition of the victory dance, while a running back named Tony Dorsett on the Dallas Cowboys scored touchdown after touchdown.

Jay put his arm around me and asked me, with a wink, what I wanted to do with my life.

I didn't blink. "I'm going to be like Dorsett!" I said. I didn't know who Dorsett was. I just wanted to be like him. I wanted my family, with Jay at it's head, to cheer for me the same way they did for Tony Dorsett.

The dream stuck. Football has been my life ever since. It's been my reason for being.

From my earliest memory of the game I've held a deep love and a natural talent for football. It felt right to me. There is nothing like the feel of the pigskin cradled in my arm. I even like the contact.

Without a football I was just another poor, lonely kid, fatherless and stuck in a town going nowhere fast. A town like too many others in America, where drugs and alcohol were eating away at the core of its youth.

The moment I tucked the ball under my arm, all that disappeared. I was *Derek Sparks,* and that meant excitement to anyone who followed the games I played. Especially in a small town with not much else going on.

One afternoon when I was 11-years-old, a pickup truck pulled into the driveway. The driver motioned to Mom. She walked over and talked for a while as I played. Suddenly I stopped. The pickup looked familiar. I'd seen it as I walked to school. It slowed sometimes while I was hanging with my friends. Sometimes it slowed near me, but always keep going.

I had never really paid much attention to the pickup truck or its driver. I was becoming used to people in town staring at me because of football.

I became curious. Who was this man Mom was talking to?

"Derek, this is your Dad," she said.

I didn't know what to say. All I could do was smile.

The man looked me up and down and asked, "How are you doing, son?"

"Fine...I guess."

I waited for something else. Nothing. I turned to Mom. Nothing. The man finally spoke, "Your mother has my phone number if you need anything." He paused. "See you around." That was it. He shut the door and backed his truck out of the driveway.

I began to notice my father's kids around school. The ones he had with his wife. They always looked sharp. New pants, new shoes. They got picked up from school by their mother in a nice car.

I learned that my father was one of the few people in Wharton who was doing well financially. But that didn't have any impact on my mom or me. Once, she took him to court for child support. I remember that members of his family testified that I wasn't his kid.

That's why I admire my mom so much, because she could have given up and handed me away to some foster family. But by the grace of God, she was able to stay strong. I love her.

One year the time arrived for all the kids to have their pictures taken by the school photographer. I really wanted my picture taken. When I asked my mom, she said we didn't have the money for that kind of thing. "But if you want to call up your dad and ask him for the money, you can."

To me, asking this man, who barely acknowledged that I was alive, for money, was the scariest thing in the world. It didn't seem like something I could possibly do.

I don't know why it meant so much to me to have my picture taken. I paced the apartment, mustered up some nerve, and called my father. He actually sounded glad to hear from me. I told him why I was calling and he said it wouldn't be a problem.

He was going to bring me the money before school, the morning the pictures were to be taken. I wanted to burst into tears of joy right then. The moment we hung up I danced around the room with unbearable excitement. I was going to see my father!

The morning of the pictures, I woke up early. I put an extra shine on my shoes and checked myself in the mirror for what seemed like a hundred times. I hopped around outside, waiting by the road for his truck.

I waited and waited, but he never showed up.

Not having a father is the way things had always been; it was always just Moms and me.

Before moving to the projects, Moms and I lived at Big Mamma's house.

3. ESCAPE

I tried for years to have some kind of relationship with my father. But trying never got me anywhere.

I called him before most of my games. "Do you think you could come, Dad?"

"Yeah," he said. "That'll be great. Seven o'clock? Okay, I'll be there."

That is as close as it ever came to any real contact. Our relationship ended with a phone call every time. Through 85 touchdowns and over 7,500 career yards, to this day, my father has never seen me play football.

My father has never made any attempt to talk about why he stood back my whole life to watch me grow up as a stranger. I wanted to ask him why he never came around. Why he never wanted to see me. Or be my dad. But I was too afraid of what he might say.

I was in a terrible position. I was afraid to hear the truth, but I couldn't deal with the lies. So I never talked to him. Even when I really needed something, monetary or otherwise, I had a hard time asking him.

Most of the time I went without. Going without things was no big deal. Over the years I became accustomed to that way of living.

There were many nights I locked myself in the bathroom for hours, crying...crying...and crying. Mom saw my bloodshot eyes and knew right away what was up. She tried to talk to me about my feelings, but there wasn't really anything either of us could say.

My spirit was broken. My self-esteem was shot. I wished I had never been born. I even thought about suicide. The only thing that stopped me was my fear of God. If I killed myself He would be upset with me. And if the suicide didn't work, Moms would have killed me.

There *was* something I could do. I could get out of Wharton. Away from my father and the pain I felt every time I thought about him and every time I saw him.

By now I was developing a pretty good name for myself on the football field. Almost everyone in town knew who I was. I had dominated virtually every game of my seventh and eighth grade seasons.

Between my backfield running mate, Omar Marks, and me, we were unstoppable. Omar was an incredible athlete. He was better than me. Omar was the team's tailback and I was the fullback. Together we comprised a formidable "I" formation.

The tailback is usually the fastest and most explosive player on a team. The fullback is a good runner and blocker, or *head hunter.* Omar was the speedster, I was the head hunter, and our games were Touchdown City. Every week during the season our names were in the local papers for miles around.

By the time we made it to the Wharton freshman team, Omar and I were in high gear. We went 9-1 that season. Our only loss was a close 22-20 score and the newspapers had a field day. One local reporter called our team *"The Omar Marks and Derek Sparks Show."* You can imagine the excitement of two ninth graders reading their names in print week after week.

My thrills, however, ended on the field. I wasn't happy living in Wharton and I became more and more restless to get out. I discovered that one of my teammates' parents had been video taping all of our games. With their help I put together a highlight video of Omar and me running over all the teams we played. It was an impressive video. It was a tunnel of escape out of Wharton and away from the ghost that haunted me. It was the video that changed my life.

*Without a football I was just
another poor, lonely kid stuck
in Wharton, going nowhere.*

4. IDENTITY

Uncle Jay was excited to get the videotape, and when he saw it he called me right away. The next call came a few days later. It was from Coach Hutchinson, the head football coach at Central High School in Long Beach, California.

I was ready to pay him to bring me out to California but that wasn't necessary. He enthusiastically told me that he would arrange for me to arrive as soon as possible. I packed my bag in a matter of minutes. I only had one.

My mother was full of reservations, but she trusted her brother Jay. They had a long talk. Jay, like me, knew that my chances of accomplishing anything in Wharton were slim. Mom knew how much this opportunity meant to me. She knew that I would miss her, but, at age 15, I was ready to go.

There was only one final piece of business I had to take care of. I had to go tell my father the news.

I walked downtown with Dante Dickerson, my childhood friend from across the street. For as long as I can remember everyone always called him "Buckwheat." I never did know why. I only knew that he always wiped his nose on his sleeve and never seemed to get in any trouble for it.

On the way through town, people shouted, "What's up Big D?"

The matrons greeted me with smiles, the girls with giggles.

"What's up, Stud?!"

No amount of approval or acceptance helped my confidence. My stomach turned over and over and Dante just wiped his nose on his shirt-sleeve while we walked.

Everyone at my father's automotive garage stared at us. It was almost like we were expected. My father came out of the office wearing his grease-stained, gray overalls, fidgeting with an oily engine part.

"Hey, it's my boy the football star!" he beamed. "What do you need son?"

"I gotta talk to you," I said.

"All right, go ahead."

"It's kind of important," I said. I hoped that he'd take me inside the garage. Somewhere that would give us some privacy.

"Yeah, I got important things going on, too. Speak up now, boy."

I blurted it out. "I'm moving to California. I'm gonna play football at one of the top schools out there...and then, maybe after that, even..."

I waited for him to say something. He remained silent for a long time, spinning that oily engine part around in his large hands. And then, he laughed. He laughed!

It wasn't a big, or even a mean laugh. But it was enough of a laugh to tell me that he thought I was joking. I was a joke. I would never amount to much.

"Let me know if you need anything," he said.

What could I say? "Yeah, thanks. I will."

That was it. I walked away with Dante at my side, still wiping his nose on his shirt. When I began to run, Dante didn't ask why. He just ran with me, all the way home.

Dante and I said our farewells later that day.

The next morning I was on a plane to a new state and a new life. I looked out of the airplane window, and tried to find Wharton in a state now the size of my palm. I let it go and said good-bye to Moms in a silent prayer.

5. THE ROAD

Central High School is where Jay's legwork and the magical highlight video-tape had landed me.

Central had one of the most powerful high school football teams in the country. It was a school that dominated its division and appeared in the city and state finals as a matter of routine.

Jay and I pulled into the Central parking lot after the 30-mile trip from his house. We sat in the van for a few minutes, observing the school through the windshield.

I couldn't believe the size of it. I wondered how so many kids could crowd into one building. But Central wasn't just one building. Acres of sprawling lawns and a city block of blacktop cement spanned a campus that was as big as a town. A huge marquee out front announced an upcoming dance. Soon my eyes focused on the one thing that was important to me: the football stadium.

There's nothing more exciting to me than walking into a football stadium for the first time. I am entering a place where special things are destined to happen.

The Central stadium wasn't all that spectacular, but to a one-horse-town Texas boy like me, it looked like Joe Robbie Stadium.

I didn't budge from the van. All of this was only a few steps away. Every dream I had, what I left home for, was before me, but I sat fidgeting in the van.

Jay smiled, looking straight through me, waiting for me to make a move. "Well, Derek, forwards or backwards?" he asked.

I didn't want to look at him and he understood my hesitation. Jay had arranged the meeting, planned the transfer, but I had to take the first actual steps. He couldn't hold my hand across the field.

"Forward or backward?" he repeated.

I stared down at my sneakers—a brand new *welcome to California* gift from Jay—the only thing about me that didn't say HICK in big bold letters.

Jay opened the door. He never said a word. I followed him to the gate and we stood there for a while, staring out at the field. I looked down at my shiny white sneakers. Jay pretended not to notice.

I stepped forward, at first slowly, feeling Jay's warm approving look. I kept walking and even felt a little swagger enter my stride; Jay a stride or two behind me.

The players were in their practice grays, running through drills. My eyes couldn't scan their practice gear fast enough. Was I at the Los Angeles Raiders camp? Workout uniforms, tackling dummies, bottles of Gatorade. Man, I was raised on tap water and Dixie cups!

Jay stood back and waited, like he had all the time in the world. I felt the butterflies starting up in my stomach. I looked at Uncle Jay, but he just stared straight ahead, watching the drills, humming a little tune to himself.

I wanted to say, "Hey man, you brought me out here. How come you don't talk to somebody?" But he never even looked at me.

I knew that Jay could take the pressure off of me any time he wanted. Jay was good with people, a persuasive talker. Not me. I always did my talking with a football. Outside of that I was a quiet, painfully shy kid.

I felt panic and a scratchiness around my eyes where tears were about to swell.

"Excuse me." Was that my voice? "I'm here to talk to Coach Kay."

The action stopped. No one moved. The entire team turned to look at me. There wasn't a sound on the field for what seemed like forever, except for the jackhammer in my chest.

They were a tough looking bunch. I had seen lots of rough looking characters back home, but none matched up to the raw edge of this group.

One huge black kid was darker than any person I'd ever seen, with big bulging purple and pink lips, and huge buck teeth that grinned and snarled at the same time.

One Hispanic linebacker reminded me of the cartoon-like pictures I'd seen years before of Mexican bandits and scoundrels.

Then there was a huge Samoan-looking monster-child who folded his arms and glowered, spitting in my direction through the gap where his front teeth had once been.

The teammates were every mix of ethnicity, but what all of these guys had in common was the look of escaped convicts, daring anyone to take them back to prison.

Someone laughed, and the rest immediately joined in. All of them were chortling; the players, coaches, the whole bunch. They didn't just laugh; they howled. Side-splitting laughter launched directly into my face.

"Aw-w-w-scyuuuse muey yau'll," twanged Purple Lips. The group broke up all over again. "Ahm haar ta towk ta Coach Kaaay." The laughter doubled.

"My name is Derek Sparks," I said above the ruckus.

The team's hysterics were turning their faces blue. They laughed so hard they couldn't breathe. This time the head coach and his assistant led the laughter.

One young assistant with a buzz cut—looking every bit the former high school quarterback—approached the head coach.

"Coach Kay, this is the kid on the video," he said seriously. "The kid on the video."

The coach and his team stood silently for a long moment. Questioning looks rippled across their faces.

"You know, THE tape!" Buzz Cut was gesturing grandly, as if the tape held the code to Fort Knox. "This is the kid who's one of that Texas two-some on THE video!"

Buzz Cut looked ready to burst. Finally, Coach Kay's eyes displayed some understanding. Of course, he had no way of recognizing me. On the video I wore a helmet and heavy pads. Besides the quality of the video, wasn't all that great, I thought, he probably got tapes from lots of kids.

It was obvious that Coach Kay was surprised to see me. He probably never believed I would show up. After all, we had had only one brief phone conversation.

Jay had first introduced me to Coach Hutchinson — the former head coach — who got fired just days before my arrival.

I didn't know at the time that both coaches who had spoken to me had committed a big time breach of regulations. I didn't know much about regulations. I didn't know much about anything.

It was Coach Hutchinson who thought my video was the greatest thing he had ever seen. He was the one who really pushed Jay to get Omar and me out to California. Hutchinson even sent us open ended airline tickets for us to visit the campus.

Coach Hutchinson made Uncle Jay feel like the sky was the limit if he could get Omar and me to attend Central. Then, when he had been suddenly fired, everything was left up in the air.

Jay showed the video to Coach Hutchinson's successor, Coach Kay. Even though Coach Kay had called me in Wharton to welcome me to try out, his excitement was nowhere near what Hutchinson's had been.

Now here I was, though, in the flesh.

"Sparks! You're a long way from home, son." Coach Kay extended his hand to me, not smiling.

"Welcome to California." He nodded briefly to Jay; a slight I couldn't help noticing. He turned to the players who were by now lounging or squatting casually on the grassy field.

"Fellas, say hello to Derek Sparks," he said casually.

Purple Lips was the first to speak. "How-deeee, Pahdnuh!"

That was all it took to send the rest of the team into another fit of laughter. Coach Kay's face turned red. Then, tight-eyed, he grew completely still. Jamming the whistle into his mouth, letting loose a long shrill blast, he screamed, "Five laps! Do it!"

"Awww coach!" the players started to complain.

"You wanna do up-downs for a hundred, first? Do it!"

That was all he needed to say. The players scattered, shooting murderous looks at me on the way.

Right then I felt like Wharton was on another planet, and I was a Whartonian. Some orange-skinned, three-headed alien with the intimidation factor of Mr. Magoo. As the players ran their laps, a smile crept onto my face. I looked over at Jay and he returned the smile. We're here.

6. Direction

"Now Derek, I want you to think about what you're doing. I want you to focus on what it is you want and what it's going to take to get there. Are you listening?"

"Uh-huh."

Jay always started his speeches with a little something about my school performance.

"You are here to get an education!"

Next came the lecture about girls.

"And forget about the girls. They don't exist for you! Girls won't do anything but distract you from your goals. ...Get you and them into nothing but trouble. You got that, D?"

"Uh-huh."

"A black man who doesn't have an education in this world ain't got a pot to piss in," he said. "In society's eyes you're special, D. Right now you're a big shot athlete, so everywhere you go people are going to make it easy for you to get by. Easier than it really is. They aren't going to make you study. They'll tell you it's okay not to go to class because they don't care what happens to you five or ten years down the line.

"They only care about your performance on the gridiron and what you can do for them and their program."

He always threw in a little history about one superstar pro athlete or another who lost it all because he didn't finish his education, and now lives under a bridge or something.

"You'll run a few touchdowns," said Jay. "Put the school on the map. Increase sales at the stadium gate, get them media attention, and get the coach a job coaching at some junior college or something. Then when your time is up they'll be too through with you. If for some reason you don't go on to play college ball, what will you have?

"Or...maybe you think since you are Derek Sparks they'll invite you for dinner and give you a decent job when you playing days are over."

"I'm going to play college ball, Jay," I said.

"You got a crystal ball in your pocket? You know what the future holds? What you're trying to accomplish is next to impossible! Sure you got talent, D, but only about one-tenth of one percent of all athletes all over the country go on to the big leagues. One-tenth of one percent. C'mon D, think about it!"

I was struggling with Jay's words. All I wanted to do was play football, score touchdowns and win games.

"Didn't they teach you anything about the real world back in Wharton? What are you going to do when the jersey comes off and your playing days are over? This is no game, D. This is serious, serious business.

"Do you really think your black butt has the same chance to make it in this messed up country as those corn-fed boys at BYU? Think again, son. Think again."

Jay didn't even stop to catch a breath. "You've enjoyed a few newspapers in a little piece-of-crap Texas town telling you that you're a big shot. All of a sudden you believe the way things have gone for two hundred years are gonna change just for you.

"Nothin' is gonna change, D. You have to change yourself. And you can't do that without an education. Do you understand me?"

I understood, but I couldn't answer. I wanted to believe that Jay felt I was going to make it no matter what. It hurt me to listen to him speculate how slim my chances were at making it in football.

I knew down deep that he was just trying to set me straight about the realities of life, but I didn't want to hear it.

"I said do you understand me?"

"Uh-huh," I said.

For a long time he looked at me. Jay had a way of doing that. Just looking, like he was trying to see deep inside me to extract more than I was willing to say. He'd stare for minutes at a time. Finally, he'd sit down next to me and throw an arm around my neck.

"Listen D, you know I believe in you." He paused. "I would never have brought you out here if I didn't. But now you're in the big city. Don't nobody give a damn about you or anyone like you, except for your family.

"You and me? We're blood. All I can do is tell you what to look out for. The rest is up to you. I wish to God I could make it easier for you. But hey, you see that carpet cleaning van sitting out there in the driveway? That's how far they let me get. And I was a great athlete too!"

Everybody at home thought for sure that Jay was going all the way. As a kid, I remember collecting everything the papers wrote about him. I could scarcely believe that Jay was my uncle. To me he was a star. The day he got drafted to play semi-pro baseball was a huge day for our whole family. I sat at home picturing him tearing up the minor leagues. I dreamed of being with him when the word came down that they needed him in the majors. The Big Show.

The word never came down from the majors, and Jay never talked about it much. They took his chance away, was the most he ever said. Like many athletes, education was always a distant second to him, and the results landed him a career in hard manual labor.

I watched him as he stared at the van in the driveway, lost in his memories. Baseball. Football. It was all the same. He was going into his home run trot, in the same stadium in which I was scoring a touchdown.

I saw just a hint of a smile on his face. A smile of satisfaction. If he could no longer touch his dream, he would make sure that I held it.

"I'll do the best I can, Jay," I said. He never answered, but I knew he heard me.

7. Practice

Stacks of crisp clothing. All kinds of top notch sporting goods and training equipment. I dressed quickly and headed out towards the field.

Everything was spinning. Every corner I turned offered a new experience of California football. It wasn't sinking in, but I couldn't take the next step fast enough. I dashed through the locker room towards the field.

Near the door was a full length mirror. I had to stop for a minute. Me, in a Central football workout uniform. I stood there for a few minutes staring into the mirror.

Some moments are hard to explain. They simply remain set apart. At that moment, I glowed.

"You gonna look at it, or get it dirty?"

Buzz Cut jarred me awake. He was teasing me, but he understood how serious I was about this day. He nodded for me to take my moment. He had once had his; it was in his face. I took a last good look and turned toward the exit. As we stepped out into the sunlight, Buzz Cut whispered, "It goes fast. Don't waste it."

While I was lost in the excitement of a new season, and this new California world, Jay and Coach Kay were having some words.

Hutchinson, made a lot of promises to Jay. Coach Kay led Jay to believe that all of those promises would, nonetheless, be delivered. But now it appeared that Coach Kay wasn't taking Jay, or me, for that matter, all that seriously.

He told Jay that, although the tape was impressive, this was Central, one of the top ranked high school football programs in the country. My age made him skeptical about whether or not I could stand up to the caliber of teams I would face.

Jay made it clear that he didn't really care about the school's football reputation. He wanted some assurance that his nephew had not flown halfway across the country for nothing. He wanted the coaches to look after my best interests.

The coach responded with a patronizing tone. "Mr. Sparks, let me tell you a little bit about our program here. We have been training young athletes in the finest tradition for many years. Many of our boys go on to play college ball. Pac-10, Big Ten and so on.

"We've had more boys turn pro than any high school in Southern California. And, I might add, we have the highest graduation rate of any high school in the district.

"Now you're new to this, and I understand your concern. But I assure you, Mr. Sparks, we are professionals. We know what we're doing. I hope I've made myself clear."

"It's very clear," answered Jay, with rivaling smugness, "that you are used to dealing with people who don't give a damn what you do with their kids. Now I'm here to tell you, Coach, that's not the case here.

"You might be able to dust off that tired recruitment speech about graduation when you're talking to other kids' parents," said Jay, "but please don't assume that you're speaking to a fool."

"Mr. Sparks..."

"Hold on Coach. Let me express myself." Jay was agitated and his speech was unrestrained.

"We both know how you folks work your graduation magic. I bet every dollar in my pocket that half of those so-called *graduates* who played ball here can hardly spell their own names.

"And it doesn't surprise me that you've had a lot of boys go on to play higher levels of football. After all, the schools recruit out here like it was the NFL. Doesn't seem to me to be too tough to build a dynasty when you ignore recruiting regulations at every turn and run your program like it was immune to the rules."

"Now hold on! You can't..."

"Coach, let's cut to the chase here." Jay continued like the coach hadn't said a word. "Derek did not call you. You called him, against just about every recruiting regulation I ever heard of. So now he's here.

"I'm sure you'd like me to just drop him off and let you do what you will with him, like you do the rest of these kids. But that's not gonna happen. If Derek Sparks is going to play ball for Central High School, you boys are going to play ball with me."

Jay paused to let it all sink in. "I know we can't follow *all* the rules and get the job done, so I'm willing to do some bending. But I'm not going to stand by and let you exploit this boy without him getting the things he needs to make a life for himself."

Coach Kay's eyebrows rose slightly. "The things he needs?"

Jay waved a hand dismissively.

"It's not like you think. I'm not gonna be asking for the kind of stuff some of these others kids' families must ask for. I'm talking about what the boy needs. We can start that list with a quality education and some assurance that you all are going take care of him.

"Of course we need to talk about his housing, transportation, school supplies, food, pocket money. Stuff like that."

"I assumed he would live with you," said Coach Kay, astonished, no doubt, at Jay's arrogance.

"Naw," said Jay. He'd have to commute every day and I don't want the boy to burn up time on the road. My wife and I don't really have much room at our place. Besides, that's the way the deal was laid out."

"Mr. Sparks, any *deal* you might have made with Coach Hutchinson is hardly..."

"You can call me Jay, Coach. And you can save your breath on this one.

"Listen, Central is the first school I contacted, and I only did that because a friend of mine told me you had a good program here. So I don't really give a damn if Derek goes here or not. All I know is, he's gonna run the football this year. Now, you decide. It can either be behind those thugs you got out there...or over them."

With that, Jay turned for the exit door and added casually, "I'll let Derek finish his workout. You should make a decision by tonight."

On the field I was hoping to create a little noise of my own. I was going to say as little as possible. I wanted to do my talking with the football. I knew the guys were just waiting for another good laugh. I wasn't going to allow that to happened.

Everything I had heard about Los Angeles was concerning the infestation of gangs. Crips, Bloods, you name it. It was clear that some of the guys on the team were in those notorious gangs. I didn't know the turf or the rules. I just knew I didn't want to cross anybody who would go off on me.

Buzz Cut and the other assistant coaches didn't waste any time putting us through the paces. After we went through our warm-up, we separated into two groups—offensive and defensive squads. Seven offensive players verses seven defensive players. The offense would run a play, sprinting into the open field, while seven defensive players pursued the ball carrier at the best angle to make the tackle.

The worst thing a defensive player can do is to let the ball carrier get outside or inside the angle of pursuit. The second worst thing, I thought to myself, would be to let this Texas boy gain some momentum.

I exploded out of my stance, received the hand-off and was off to the races.

I saw where the defenders positioned themselves, and I almost chuckled.

C'mon fellas, I'm just a country Texas kid. How could I have the speed to turn this corner on you?

I heard them closing in. About five yards to the sideline, I cut back toward the field with a head and shoulders move. I could see the defensive back break his stride.

There goes one.

I shifted back outside. Here comes the safety. I gave him a little move, rocking my head from side to side, just enough to make him hesitate. I accelerated to the outside, and left him around mid-field bumping into another defensive back as I scooted up field to the end zone.

The rest of the team didn't react. They just grew quiet and shared looks with each other out of the corners of their eyes. I didn't say a thing. I simply let the ball drop in the end zone and jogged back to the huddle.

The second and third carries took no thinking at all. They had no idea what kind of speed I had, so I simply out-ran them. Like a ritual, I let the ball drop and roll on the grass. After my third carry, on the way back to the huddle, I heard one of the defenders say, "F*** you, Hayseed!"

I wasn't going to let that affect me. I was just getting warmed up. It was one of those days where the small gaps on the field appeared huge and every move I needed to make felt like the easiest thing in the world. I sensed the confusion of some of the team members. They hadn't expected this.

The assistant coaches were blasting the defensive backs for blowing their assignments. All but Buzz Cut. He was wearing a smug smile. I had the feeling that at least someone was pulling for me.

The defense was gearing up to make me pay for those last three carries. I had to be careful. We were in tee-shirts, shorts, and helmets; no pads, and no protection against injury. I had seen players miss an entire season because of a wrong move or a cheap shot, and I wanted no part of that.

The showdown was on. With every carry, my jersey fit a little better. My adrenaline was pumping. My legs were responding. The defense found themselves pulling chunks of grass and mud from their face-masks. Maybe my drawl vanished. Nobody seemed to be making fun of me anymore.

On the way home Jay and I hardly exchanged a word. I was busy trying to put everything into perspective and he was busy contemplating something. I didn't know what.

We pulled into the driveway. Jay's wife waved from the doorway.

"It's for you, Jay. The phone. It's Coach Kay from Central High." Jay slowly got out of the van without looking at me.

I sat there, thinking all the time he was on the phone. I thought about how scared I was when I walked onto the Central field. I thought about how incredible I felt on the field. I knew, in truth, that I had been fortunate that those guys underestimated me. As a fullback, I had unlikely skills for my size, and they had never seen my moves before. Good timing, good fortune. I didn't care. It felt good.

Thirty minutes must have gone by while I sat in the van, thinking. Jay got back into the van and broke my daydream as he reclined back in the driver's seat.

"What the hell did you do out there today, D?" he screeched.

My heart sank. I tried to think of what I had done wrong. I did the best I could. I moved as fast as I ever had. I worked as hard as I was capable of working. Maybe I had hurt a player on defense, but everyone had been out to hurt me.

"What do you mean?" I asked defensively.

"You showed your behind out there today, boy." Jay broke into peels of laughter. "They just about lost their minds over you." He was bouncing in his seat and pounding the dashboard. "That coach is about ready to drive out here and stand guard outside your bedroom door to make sure nobody else gets to you. You did it, D!"

I felt a rush of relief. "What'd I do?" I asked meekly.

"It's all set up," said Jay. "The whole enchilada. That's what you did!

Your man, the coach, is singing a new tune." He went into a bad imitation of Coach Kay.

"We feel that Central High has a lot to offer a young man like Derek. Although he's inexperienced, we'd like to take a chance on him."

"Take a chance?" My head was spinning.

"...A chance to kiss your backside!" Jay shouted.

He couldn't control himself. He was laughing and crying. Holding his sides. Bouncing in his seat and convulsing to the point where he couldn't speak.

I didn't understand the big joke, but I was relieved to hear that I had found a team in California. So, I laughed too.

The two of us sat in that van for the longest time; laughing, talking, and laughing some more.

8. RITUAL

On game day every athlete has a different ritual. Steps or routines they perform to prepare for the game. Some people call it a game face. Some call it getting in the zone.

For me, it's *the ritual.*

It starts with music.

Throughout my career I've always kept some kind of CD or cassette player close and handy on game day.

I put on my headphones and crank it up. BeBe and CeCe Winans or Anita Baker. Some kind of music that feels spiritual to me. Allowing the Holy Spirit to rumble in my soul. Before I go to battle, I want to wake up the Spirit. I try to get lost in the music.

I always try to be the first one on the bus. That way I can choose my seat. Something far away from the guys who get loud or like to horse around before a game. I don't mind them messin' around. Every player has a different way of getting where he needs to be before a game.

Some guys like to bang their head against lockers. Some lift weights. Some guys get stoned on marijuana or cocaine. That's their way. My way is ...quiet. I don't have anything to say to anybody. On game day, I let the music do all the talking.

During the bus trip or airplane ride I stare out of the window and think about the things expected of me during the game.

Because I sit in the front of the bus, when we arrive at the stadium, I'm the first one into the locker room. I find myself a corner locker, far away from the action. The music is driving me now. It's driving me into a condition of quiet confidence and relaxed excitement. I drop my bags in front of the locker and move quickly to the training room so I can be the first to get taped.

Taping is serious business. When I am on the field—cutting, breaking and pivoting—I have to know that my feet and ankles have enough support. If an athlete rolls an ankle at the wrong moment, it's over. I learned, early on, that taping is as important as the protective gear. That's why I make it a point to get the same trainer each time.

I watch closely to make sure the trainer's technique is correct. The tape feels just right.

The music is still cranking in my head. *"Hold up the light!"* I'm taking it all in, watching the roll of tape go around one ankle again and again.

There might be 30- or 45-minutes before we take the field, but I'll just sit there in front of my locker staring at the wall. In a trance, I visualize myself breaking tackles and running one in for the score. I wait about 15-, maybe 20-minutes, until it is time for the team to go out to the field.

Then I get into my gear.

Socks...hip pads...thigh pads...knee pads...tailbone pad...pants...cleats, double knot each...shoulder pads...jersey...wristbands...mouth guard...game towel. Tape down all the parts that might stick out, giving a defender something to grab.

Now the rest of the team is really getting pumped. They're banging each other on the pads, smashing their helmets together, hollering, piling onto each other, whatever.

I'm still in a corner with my headphones. *"Hold up the light! Save the world from darkness!"*

Now it's time to hit the field, and I'm ready. I put the music aside and finally begin to jump up and down, pumping myself up, getting the blood flowing. The rest of the team is already fired up.

Some of the players have spent the whole week with aches and pains. At this moment, with the help of pain killers or a cortisone shot from the team physician (I call him the magic man behind the white curtain), they are feeling no pain.

Just like hundreds of times before, my mind starts to ask my body to deliver. And so far, thanks be to God, my body has always come through.

I make contact with my teammates, the men whom I will go into battle with, whom I will depend on to watch my back, to open holes, to push me forward. We work ourselves into a frenzy and hit the field.

Although excitement fills the air, my body feels no tension. The team goes into stretching drills. Just like before, on the bus, I am completely still. No yelling or growling. I analyze my body, flexing and prodding each muscle until I'm convinced that it is a fine piece of artillery ready for combat.

At this moment, my mind begins to betray me.

We run to the sidelines for the team huddle and I look to the player running next to me. He has no pads on. I look closer. It's Dante Dickerson, my childhood friend from across the street in Wharton, Texas. Dante smiles and wipes his nose on his shirt-sleeve.

I look into the stands. There are no fans or spectators. Just a few people from my father's automotive garage.

I shake my head to clear the cobwebs and once again I hear the screams of the stadium crowd. The coach is saying something, something inspirational, but I can't hear it. The shouts of the crowd are inside of me.

As we take the field for the opening kickoff, my body knows what to do, but my mind is still in doubt. The cheers of the crowd sound like laughter.

I glance to the stands to check it out. Then I see *him.* He is sitting in the front row. He's wearing gray, grease-covered overalls, the oily engine part still in his hands, a cheap cigar in his mouth. The rest of the people in the stands are cheering. All I hear are the words of this stranger from my past, around inside my helmet.

The kickoff is underway. I feel as though my head will burst from all of the sounds...the screaming crowd, my father's laughter. For a moment I am unsure, but my body knows what to do.

I cradle my arms into position and catch the rotating falling object from the sky. My hands grasp the only thing that I can trust. The only thing that brings me comfort. I clutch the football tight to my chest. Now I am sure.

9. THE DEAL

I admit I was a naive country boy. I didn't know nothin' from nothin'. I left everything in Jay's hands and simply prepared to play football the best I could. I didn't know much about what was legal and what wasn't; how things should or shouldn't go down. I only knew one thing: I wanted to stay in California and continue my journey toward my dream, playing football in the NFL.

The "deal" at Central was enough to make this small town boy feel like he had arrived. Coming from Wharton, I was happy that I'd been given any attention or perks. I didn't think about whether these gifts were given to me in keeping with the rules or not. It never even crossed my mind.

The first part of the deal was my living arrangements. When I showed up at practice on the second day, the coaches sent Jay over to talk to one of the boosters who had dropped by the field. As it turned out, this guy owned an apartment complex right across the street from the school. What a coincidence. He would work it out so Jay's name would be on the lease.

"We can't have a 15-year-old kid living by himself," the man said. But that's exactly what did happen.

Every morning, I woke up, put on my clothes, ate some breakfast and walked across the street to school. Every now and then Jay stopped by to check on me, but his carpet cleaning business kept him busy.

The coaching staff, taking regular turns, stopped by to check on me. One coach made sure the cupboards and the refrigerator were filled with groceries. Another coach dropped in to make sure that the food was something I could easily prepare.

Pots, pans and silverware were all provided, along with linen and household furnishings. Things just got taken care of.

The coaches—my benefactors—came through with bundles and bags and a little conversation. Was I all right? Did I need anything? Then, they'd be gone.

Jay paid as much of the rent for the apartment as he could. The rest of it, I don't know. It just got taken care of.

It seemed like there was always somebody--a coach, a booster or alumnus coming up to me, shoving twenty bucks into my pocket, saying, "Let me know if you need anything."

I quickly learned to play the game. When I wanted new tennis shoes, game-related or not, I went to the coaches' office and said, "Coach, I need some sneakers."

On the same day, by practice time, I had a couple boxes of shoes in my locker. Things just got taken care of.

The coaches took interest in everything I did. Every other day it seemed that one of them was asking me how I was doing in my classes.

That's code for: *Which teachers do we need to talk to?*

I never asked for any grade consideration; it was simply how the machine worked for star athletes at Central High. Things were always taken care of.

I don't mean to sound like I didn't want the attention. I wanted all of it! I was a dirt poor Texas kid who had never had much of anything. If somebody was going to give me an allowance, there was no way I was going to refuse it.

Even as a young kid in Wharton, people were nice to me because I was a good athlete. As far as I was concerned, this was the way it was supposed to be. If I did my job and stood out as a player, people made sure I had the things I wanted. Not the things I needed.

I was only 15-years-old. I was an immature student-athlete being treated like a professional. The coaches didn't have a problem with it. Uncle Jay didn't have a problem with it. And no, I didn't have a problem with it either.

Looking back, I see that it was wrong. It was wrong, but I was just a kid, like a lot of other kids then and now. Young athletes are offered gifts with huge hidden price tags. If they knew the price, they'd never accept.

A coach's perspective can get myopic. They're looking up the ladder, like everybody else, peering up at their future opportunities. Win, win, win. Perform, perform, perform, or the student athlete is cut. He is expendable.

I knew I was living well, but I wasn't looking past the stereo and the big-screen television set.

There were too many people acting selfishly. Somebody was bound to get hurt.

Uncle Jay began to have problems with the allowances being made in regard to my academic pursuits. He had run-in after run-in with the coaches.

"We'll take care of that, Mr. Sparks," was their answer to all of his questions. Little progress was ever made.

All I wanted was to make myself an important part of the team. And let me tell you, this was a tough team to stand out on. The guys who were ahead of me at the running back position had ripped up the league the year before.

This year they were expected to lead Central High to the city championship.

Central also had a bunch of other players who looked like they would go on to play some serious football after high school. Bobby Winfield was being hyped up as one of the best lineman in the country.

None of my teammates made it easy for me to just walk on the field and be accepted. They teased me, calling me "Hayseed," "Gomer" and "Rookie." Once we got into pads, they never missed a chance to rib me, to see how far they could push me.

I took their best shots without a word. And I dished out a few pretty good licks of my own. I hung in there and tried to do everything asked of me by the coaches and my teammates.

The focus of my fear was on Purple Lips. I knew that he was one of the players who was heavy into the gang scene. I didn't want to get on his bad side. He was a Piru, a part of the Blood gang, the mortal enemy of the Crips (of which there were a few on the team), but they had some kind of on-field truce worked out.

Purple Lips was hard-core. He called everybody *blood*. Except me. He called me "pigsucker." Relentlessly. It started getting to me. I wanted the respect of my teammates, which is hard to earn when they all busted up laughing every time this guy called me *pigsucker*.

This all swam in my head during one particular one-on-one drill. We were running a play called "Tailback Lead Draw." I was at fullback with the assignment of laying a block on the middle linebacker.

Of course on this play it had to be Purple Lips I was blocking. He was a tough customer. Since I was a running back, he expected me to give him some kind of cross body block where I'd roll and take his legs out from under him.

I knew he'd be waiting and would hurdle me, easily making the tackle. If that happened, he'd think I was soft and the coaches would be all over me. So my choice was dealing with the coaches or dealing with *The Lips*. It was not an easy decision.

The play opened with me leading. I could tell Purple Lips had read the play, and as I crossed the line of scrimmage, I could see him in hot pursuit.

I ducked my head a little, as if to get ready to lunge at his legs. Right at that moment, I readjusted and planted my feet, giving him the best shot under his chin that I had given in some time.

It made my ears ring, I hit him so hard. He went down in a heap, and I could tell he was rocked. For a few seconds he was out. The play was over. As we jogged back to the huddle, Purple Lips tried to pull himself together.

"Hey!," he shouted. "Who the hell do you think you are?"

I stopped and steeled myself. "Sparks," I said.

The whole field fell silent, and moaned, waiting for Purple Lips to try and split me in half.

Instead, he grinned at me. "Nice hit, Sparks. But you're still a pig-sucker."

No. I was a Central Cougar.

Playing
Central
football
was an
awakening.

10. CENTRAL

Preparations for the first season at Central High are a blur in my mind. One jumbled memory of playbooks, passing leagues, hitting drills, shaking hands, conditioning, conditioning, conditioning. I loved every minute of it!

The coaches were pleased with me, but they were pleased with a lot of guys. We had talent. Keith Walker and Kenny Sims were penned as the starting running backs. That made sense. They were both seniors, highly touted, and had paid their dues.

A part of me felt relief. Keith, the fullback, was a hard-core Crip and I didn't want trouble with any gangbangers. I figured that broken bones and bullet wounds would hinder my performance. The gang violence of California was a cautionary tale back in Wharton, Texas, and I was fearing the consequences if I took this guy's starting spot.

Gangs, or no gangs, I was glad to be at Central.

I'll never forget the day of the first game. Although I wasn't expeced to see any action, and I was riding the pine, no one would have known it to look at me. I felt like a kid in a candy store. I went through my usual pre-game ritual, trying to reach a condition of calm; but man, I was excited.

When I put on my game uniform for the first time, I felt electric. My face lit up. Brand new—red and black. I looked over at my teammates and wondered how we looked to the outside world. The uniforms seemed to catch and reflect every color, every image in the stadium. We looked like champions.

When we ran down the tunnel, I heard the crowd. That was it. I've heard raucous fans before, but this was big time. Central was a serious football school. It was obvious that the people who came to these games, came to be heard.

I was in a daze all through the stretching drills. Before I knew it, the opening kickoff was in the air. I don't remember much about the game, aside from running up and down the sidelines to cheer on my teammates. I didn't see any action; we won 25-10 and I left the field with the same feeling of excitement I had entered with.

Then, it happened.

Our second game, as the clock ticked towards the final moments, Keith went down hard. He had twisted his ankle. He tried to shake it off but I could tell it was bad. Somehow he finished the game but he was hurting in the locker room.

I just wanted to get out of there. I didn't want to be some vulture, hanging around, waiting to see if I could claim the carcass. I hoped he'd be okay. I would never want a player, opponent, or teammate gloating at my injury. Nobody deserves that. I've seen freak injuries take away a young man's dream too many times.

It turned out Keith's injury was serious. The coaches called my apartment early the next day. They were all over me.

"All right Derek. This is what you been waiting for. This is your chance to step up and prove that you belong on the varsity team," said Coach Kay. "Show everyone out here that you are for real."

"I'm starting?"

"This week, against Muir," he said. "Muir is ranked in the top five in the city polls. You're our fullback. You're going to get us there. Can you go?"

I knew he was trying to get me pumped for the game. I also knew the minute Keith came back they would throw me back on the bench.

"I can go," I said.

"That's good, Derek. That's real good." He paused. "We need you to pay extra attention in the team meetings and film sessions. Your practices have to be sharp and crisp. You're in the starting lineup for Central High School now. You know what that means?"

"I think I do," I said.

"We know you won't let us down."

◆◆◆

The following week of practice was a whole new situation for me. I was the guy the coaches needed, so everything was "Derek, how do you feel?" "You're the man, Derek."

Even my teammates treated me differently. They still made fun of my accent but it almost became a bond of friendship. It gave them a kick to simply think about it.

"Derek, would you talk for us?"

I would say a sentence or two, and they would just go crazy. I could say *dishwater* and they would fall down laughing. I wondered if all Southerners were as funny as I was.

The guys were behind me. A word here, a look there, a few slaps on the helmet. They were beginning to believe in me.

When I told Jay I was the starter he smiled and hugged me. This shocked the heck out of me because Jay wasn't a hugger. He motioned for me to sit.

"I'm sure you've thought about all of this, but this is what you came here for. This is what it's all about. All the training and sacrifice. All of it.

"The only person who can stop you, is you. Nobody expects you to go out there and score a touchdown every time you touch the ball. They do expect you to go out there and play your game. Just like on the highlight video. Nothing different.

"Just work hard, keep your head in the game, do what you do best. Everything else will take care of itself. I'm proud of you D," he smiled. "Now go call your mama."

I did. Mom was really excited, although I'm not sure she knew exactly what a big deal it was. She knew I was happy and that was enough for her. The rest of the family got on the line to wish me luck. It felt good.

I didn't bother to call my father.

Funny as it may sound, none of this made me nervous. I had lost the fear of playing football a long time before, even in a high stakes game. I was just excited to have a shot. I had always felt comfortable on the field, and this time was not different. Not one bit.

Okay, a little bit.

I admit that the butterflies found their way into my stomach on game day. We traveled to play John Muir at a college stadium in Los Angeles. It was a night game, held under the lights. I sat alone at my locker; various team members and coaches came by to offer encouragement. I heard nothing except my music, BeBe and CeCe Winans. *"No weapons formed against me shall prosper."* I was deep in my own thoughts, processing the job ahead of me.

Coming out of the tunnel, onto the field, I scanned the stadium and was in awe. I had no idea how many fans traveled to see a high school football game. Spectators jammed the bleachers. The stadium lights intensified the excitement. The noise was deafening as we ran onto the field.

John Muir won the coin toss to see who would control the ball first. I'd have to wait a little longer to make my starting debut. Kenny Sims would still be the tailback. Fine, I played the fullback position in front of Omar in Texas and I was comfortable there. When we took the field I was ready.

We ran a "34 Veer Option."

On our second possession, I got the call. Kenny would swing as if we were running the "34 Veer Option" again. Instead of faking like I had the ball, I would actually take the hand-off and run off-tackle.

The ball was snapped. I exploded towards the line of scrimmage. I couldn't believe the size of the hole Bobby Winfield opened up for me. I wanted to stop and thank him. All I needed was for the defensive end to buy Kenny's fake long enough to give me a step. He gave me about half of one. I burst through the hole.

The over-pursuing linebacker moved quickly to recover. I took it straight to him, helmet to helmet. As we collided, I bounced off of him and he fell back just enough to give me some space up-field. Out of the corner of my eye I saw another defender moving to take me out. But before I knew it, our tight end, Mark Fields, had kissed him goodnight and I shifted into high gear. As I moved into the secondary, I saw two defensive backs from my peripheral vision as I cut to the outside.

Then I let it flow. Like the first day of practice.

One defensive back ate nothing but the grass. The other tripped. I cruised into the end zone untouched, for a 40-yard touchdown. My first touchdown as a Central Cougar!

The crowd went crazy, looking around at each other, asking, "Who was that?" I crossed the goal line, let my arms fall to my sides, and allowed the football to roll in the end zone.

When I reached the sideline, my teammates swarmed me. The first person to grab me was Purple Lips. His crooked teeth poked though those huge, dark lips.

"That's it. You ain't no pigsucker, boy. From now on, your name is *Showtime.*"

From that day forward, by decree of Purple Lips, all of my teammates referred to me as *Showtime.* The media eventually picked it up, and the name stuck.

I rushed over to thank Winfield and Fields for the key blocks. I meant it. We carried our momentum through the rest of the game and came out on top.

Jay ran down to the field after the game. He shook my hand, congratulated me, and said he was proud. I tried my best to remain stoic and not come off like a glory hound. Before he could finish, a frenzy of reporters broke up the team. They circled around me, fired off questions, and elbowed each other for room. They caught me off guard as I tried to absorb all of their questions at once. I caught a glimpse of Jay who surveyed this spectacle with a huge grin on his face. Then he nodded to me and I couldn't help but smile.

11. THE HYPE

As far back as I can remember, my name has been in the newspapers on a regular basis. Post good numbers and get the media's attention. It's that simple. It was just like my developing relationship with the high school's sports machine. Post good numbers, things get taken care of.

It was an unusual way to grow up, always reading about yourself, seeing your picture in the paper. But for me, even at 13- and 14-years-old, it was a way of life.

I have to admit, it was exciting to wake up on Sunday morning, run down to the newsstand and grab all the local papers.

I opened one after the other, going through them and reading what the local reporters had to say about me. I began to develop a rapport with most of them. I even thought of a few of the reporters as pretty good friends. It was a false assumption.

When times got tough, *friendships* flew out the window. I soon learned that they wrote whatever made the best story.

From those early days at Central High, to my last days of high school football, I couldn't believe the way I was painted by the media. Although most of the sports reporters knew me and had interviewed me many times, when they smelled the hint of a scandal, they issued their articles and editorials based on rumor and speculation.

The fact is, I attended four different schools in four years. It didn't take a whole lot of kindling for these reporters to turn innuendo into a blazing controversy. Fans would heckle me based on what they'd read in those articles; but this was just the beginning.

At Central, the media reporters were my friends. Later, their significance in my life and the tenacity of their efforts would reach a level I could never have anticipated.

I began running into more and more press. Keith, my backfield competition, recovered quickly but the coaches told him they wanted him to rest up; make sure he was completely healthy. That's how they let him know I was the new fullback. Keith saw what was going on. He didn't like it.

Keith knew that as a senior, he couldn't rest on his past success; every game counted towards a scholarship. A scholarship he hadn't yet landed. Now he saw himself on the way out, making room for the younger player, a new rising star.

He read the papers and knew there was a lot of ink tabbing me as the next great running back. His resentment seemed to grow with each article.

I tried to stay out of it. I had nothing to say to anybody. I was just praying that Keith wouldn't fly into a rage and visit me with a bunch of his homeboys. Keith was a good guy but he was a straight up gangsta. There were too many stories circulating. Shootings, fights, things I wanted no part of.

I felt bad about what was happening to him. I saw him as another case of a young black athlete with tunnel vision, pinning his hopes on football to help him rise above his socio-economic condition.

The coaches and advisors had told him again and again, "Just run the football. Work hard, be at practices on time, score touchdowns, and everything will get taken care of."

But the nature of sports is: Someone gets hurt, and someone else steps up to fill the gap. Suddenly the team doesn't remember you or what you've accomplished on the field.

For Keith, it was the last chance to post some numbers. Numbers mean scholarships, which, for a guy like Keith, was all the difference between going or not going to college.

Keith handled it the wrong way. He developed a terrible attitude. He went off on the coaches. He dogged it in practice and violated every team rule he could think of.

I guess he figured *"What difference does it make if I bust my hump?"* He saw that there was no reward for following the rules. So he made up his own rules and became impossible to deal with. When the coaches had had enough, they called him in and he was gone. Just like that.

Keith's problem was all too common, I'm afraid. The hard truth is, many kids hurt themselves beyond anything the coaches or anyone else could do to them. They get wrapped up in the game and don't make any effort in school. Classes don't hold much reward for a star athlete who is enjoying the immediate rewards and splendor of his sport. Keith was a football player, not a student. He was taught to build his body rather than his mind. He allowed things to be taken care of. Until the day things weren't taken care of. This happens all the time.

The season went on as if Keith never existed and I became the starting fullback. I set out to prove that I was for real. It didn't take a genius to see that if I faltered for a minute, I would be replaced by someone hungrier than I was for the chance to run the football. So, I played as hard as I could.

Meanwhile, every Sunday I headed down to the newsstand:

A YOUNG SPARK RIDES IN FROM TEXAS

A Texan takes over Cougar Town. He lassoes a starting position on the football team. He rounds up some touchdowns from Mohicans and Mustangs...

SPARKS FLIES FOR CENTRAL

Central High sophomore running back Derek Sparks had a coming out party Friday afternoon, rushing for 199-yards and four scores to lead the visiting Cougars (6-0)(8-1) to a 34-14 win over Crenshaw (4-2)(5-3).

COUGARS HAVE EASY TIME WITH MANUAL ARTS

Central's first round L.A. city football playoff game was an exercise in futility for Manual Arts, and well, just an exercise for the Cougars.

...Cougars fullback Derek Sparks had the other second half touchdown for Central on a 2-yard run. He was the leading rusher for the game with 136 yards on 16 carries. He played just a little more than a half...

SPARKS KEEPS ELECTRICITY IN COUGAR'S RUNNING GAME

Think of Central High football, and you can't help but think of the great running backs who have passed through the school.

The Cougar's ball-carrying alumni include two-time L.A. City Player of the Year Stan Wilcox (Cincinnati Bengals), former UCLA star Freeman Mack (New York Jets), rugged fullback Mark Alan (ex-USC), speedster Dan Andrews (ex-UCLA), and USC's current fullback, powerful Leroy Hoard.

Derek Sparks could be the next player to join that illustrious list.

Central's sophomore fullback is only 15-years-old, but already he's showing the talent that could earn him a major scholarship as a senior.

"...he's incredible." the coach said. "He could have had a 300-yard night against Crenshaw, but we only played him for one series in the second half. I think we're capable of winning the city championship if he keeps having games like he's been having.

With these headlines came the opportunity I had dreamed of for all of my short life. The headlines were a reinforcement of why I came to California. We had played powerfully as a team and I had surpassed even my own goals as a player. The reward was here, in the *Los Angeles Times...*

...tonight Derek, and his teammates, will play before 20,000 to 30,000 fans on a field where the pros and big time collegians play...

"Not too many 15-year-olds get to do this," said Sparks. "This will be my first time playing in a game this big."

Bill Inch/Press-Telegram

Central High running back Derek Sparks stands tall when he's with his offensive line. The 15-year-old leads Cougars in City championship against traditional rival Carson tonight at Coliseum.

12. THE MOMENT

The Los Angeles Coliseum. I couldn't believe it. The site where the 4-A City Championship game was to be played.

We were on a collision course with a monster team, the Carson Colts. They defeated us in the regular season, 24-13, and now we were fighting, once more, for bragging rights. We knew the battle ahead, but these are the battles an athlete lives for. We acted and felt like a bunch of caged animals, scraping and snarling, until the first snap was hiked on the Coliseum grass.

For twenty years it has always been Carson and Central. When people talked about high school football in Southern California, these two schools dominated the conversation. A strong tradition weighed on this final game. It meant a lot to the supporters and people affiliated with both programs.

The first time I ever visited California, Jay took me down to see the L.A. Coliseum. Jay was living in Los Angeles and I was just a little kid. We stood in front of that huge arena and got a stranger to take our picture. I let my mind dance.

Look at this field. So this is what the grass feels like. I hear the crowd cheering. I make a cut over there, race up the sideline..."Touchdown, D. Sparks!"

We stood there for a long time as our minds covered every inch of the field at light speed. For one entire tourist afternoon my whole world rested within those Coliseum walls.

Now, that day had truly come.

I sat back in my seat while the world outside the team bus rocked in chaos, as a dozen or so police motorcycles escorted us onto the stadium grounds.

As we approached the stadium, a hostile mob of what looked like Carson supporters chanted obscenities. Out of nowhere there was a loud blast and a crashing sound in the bus. Come to find out, someone had thrown a bottle, violently hitting the bus. No arrests were made, but it only proved to me that the history of bad blood between the two high schools was alive and well.

The police motorcycles that had escorted us to the stadium now surrounded our bus. I pondered why someone would build this world-renowned stadium in the heart of the ghetto. I sat back in my seat and tried to regain my focus.

The game was being televised citywide and USC's Heisman trophy winner, Mike Garrett, was calling the play by play. All of this was a testimony to L.A.'s claim as the sports capital of the world.

Dreams sometimes take disappointing turns. They mauled us, 56-7, on a night where everything went wrong. Carson had an arsenal of great players and coaches. It was like they took turns scoring touchdowns, just to be gracious to each other.

They shut me down too. I gained 133 yards. But they were ugly yards. I only sniffed the end zone once.

The Cougars boarded the bus that night buried in a sea of disappointment. I felt bad for the seniors, especially the ones who played their last football game ever! The loss tore straight through me, but I couldn't shake another thought in my head.

It felt strange and refused to leave. After a while I gave up and allowed the feeling to take over. I leaned back and watched the city pass through the window for the rest of the trip. One stubborn notion distracted me from my sadness. *I'll be back, I'll be back, I'll be back...*

The highlight of my first trip to California, with my cousin Preston, was our trip to the L.A. Coliseum.

13. CENTRAL TENSION

"Derek, this is an important time for you. Every game you've got to play heads up. You can't let down, Big D. We've got plans for you." Coach Kay was becoming my best friend.

"Top college teams are going to start keying in on you. You can't get caught napping and let everybody think you were just a flash in the pan.

"Keep working hard. Keep yourself out of trouble and you'll have a chance to become one of the greatest running backs this city has ever known. But you can't get too relaxed.

"You're not there yet, and you've got a lot to learn. But we're all committed to you, and if you hang in there you'll be on your way to whatever college you want to play for, and then on into the pros."

It sounded good but I couldn't focus too hard on what the coach was saying. Even while Coach Kay was talking to me I pictured Keith Walker listening to the same pitch the year before. Where was he now?

My value to the coaches was directly connected to my ability to run the football. Take that away and they'd be singing a whole different tune.

For the moment though, I was the guy. I was named *Herald Examiner* **Player of the Week** and the *Daily Breeze's* **All-Area First Team**. I was the youngest player to be named to the All-City team. A number of national publications listed me as one of the fifty top underclassmen to watch and rated me as one of the most eligible college recruits in the country. And I was only a sophomore!

I received a flood of interest from major universities. Included among these universities were the two schools I dreamed of as a kid, USC and UCLA.

I was in the top five in almost every offensive statistical category in the city. As if all of this wasn't enough, one morning I received a phone call from Coach Kay, with the news that had been named California State Sophomore Player of the Year.

Out of all the great running backs who had played for Central High, this had never been done. I was on my way! I thanked God for Uncle Jay and for giving me this opportunity. I also whooped and yelled around the apartment for what seemed like hours.

◆◆◆

I received an envelope in the mail that week. There was no return address but I sensed that it was performance related. Was a one-hundred dollar bill performance related? Maybe it was a gift from the machine.

It was an incredible year. As I pocketed the contents of the envelope I thought, *I'm on my way.*

Everyone at school treated me better and better as the weeks went by. Kids I didn't know waved and called my name. Teachers stopped to ask me how everything was going. Administrators introduced me to visitors, and I noticed girls looking at me all the time.

I remembered Jay's warning, but I had to smile back. I wasn't stupid!

Jay, in the midst of all of this good stuff, wasn't happy with my situation at Central. From the beginning, he felt the coaches weren't taking him seriously. They were looking at him as a crazy uncle and armchair football coach.

There was a perpetual argument between Jay and the coaches as to whom I should listen to; who knew what was best for me.

Jay stayed on Coach Kay about pulling me out of games too soon. Kay argued that there was no sense exposing me to injury if a game was out of reach. "Besides," he argued, "we're not here to humiliate the weaker teams in the league."

Jay fumed. The coaches were holding me back, he said. They were keeping my numbers down so recruiters and other people (me included) wouldn't know yet how good I really was. This would eliminate any threat of losing me to another high school program.

The coaches' negligence towards my education was Uncle Jay's central complaint. "They have no problem talking to one of your teachers when you fall behind in a class," he said. "What they need to be doing is getting you some help."

It was true. If a choice was left to them whether I should work out or go to class, then there was no choice. My teachers would just as soon give me the grade.

Jay wanted them to push me to keep my grade point average up. He knew they considered good grades to be unnecessary. If I kept running the football the way I had, I'd have no trouble running my way into a scholarship offer and then on to the NFL.

If I couldn't deliver, they'd have no use for me. I could be somebody else's problem. This scenario drove Jay insane and he refused to relent.

Jay was not getting what he had been promised when the deal was sealed. When Jay first made contact with Coach Hutchinson, before he was fired, Hutchinson made it sound like Jay's input would be welcomed and valued. He told Jay that the school would work with him to bring other talented kids out from Texas, and provide them with a chance to escape Wharton and build a future.

You remember Omar, my running mate from the freshman team in Texas?

I didn't know at the time, that they wanted Omar Marks worse than they wanted me. They flew him and my cousin, Preston Sparks, a talented receiver at Wharton High, in for a workout and to check things out just a week or two before the season started.

Jay was wary of the Central coaches using him to obtain all of these talented kids, only to shove him aside. The way he saw things was that the coaches wanted one hundred percent control of their athletes. Mind, body, and soul. They wanted our allegiance. We were there to always do what was best for the program. Even at our own expense. Jay wasn't having it.

When Omar and Preston visited and worked out with the Central team, I couldn't mask my excitement. I felt in my heart that if these boys were given a new start in California, they would both go all the way to the top. They were incredible athletes.

In the end though, Omar's mom made him go back to Texas. She didn't want him out in that crazy Hollywood scene. Omar was heartbroken, but he had to obey his mother. Central lost a great player that day.

My cousin Preston was another story. Jay always said that Preston was a truly gifted athlete, but his laziness would be his downfall.

"See Derek," he explained, "Preston doesn't have the same drive or determination that you have. If Preston were out here, you could help him along."

Uncle Jay wanted Preston to stay for his career. I wanted him to stay for his own sake. Our home situations were almost identical and we were both hurting in a lot of ways. Besides, Preston was family. And even though I had football and school to keep me busy, I was lonely. Preston and I grew up together. We were like brothers. If Preston was at Central we could look after each other like the old times back in Wharton.

We were both broken up when, just days after he got here, Preston got a phone call from his mother telling him that she needed him to come home. She and Preston's father were trying to work out the terms of their divorce and she needed Preston to be in her custody. He was gone.

Jay hinted that Preston went home because he didn't want *it* enough. *It* was the dream. "And that," he whispered somberly, "was too bad."

I think the coaches felt Jay didn't try hard enough to convince Omar and Preston to stay.

Jay explained to them that he wasn't about to hold a gun to kids' heads and tell them to leave home. It had to be a decision made by them and their parents.

Jay had plenty of ideas to help young men—those who were outstanding athletes—influencing them to become productive citizens, and he didn't mind crossing the coaches to do it.

What started as a smoldering slight now seared inside of him, as no one at the school took him seriously. He constantly laid his hand before the coaches. "I put Derek in this school, and I can take him out," he'd say.

To the coaches, this equated to messing with the lion's dinner. Jay was a threat. He was an irrational threat. The coaches did everything to shut him out; at the same time doing everything they could to lock me in, making sure I never brewed any funny ideas about relocating.

At one point they actually had a coach move into the apartment with me, just to provide them with surveillance. I stayed under the Central microscope around the clock.

Hey, I didn't mind. It meant that my chaperon could pay for whatever I might need or wanted around the house. This man was Coach White.

White was a huge, black former athlete who came in with all this stereo equipment, big screen TV, appliances and you name it.

I didn't know who was paying for all of this, I just knew that the big screen was a really big screen.

From time to time one of the boosters or someone stopped by and asked Coach White, "How's Derek doing?" White always answered, "Oh, great. He's doing just fine."

Then they'd slip a few twenties in his pocket. Steak dinner that night!

And you know what? That was all good with me. I just figured the machine was operating accordingly and I was in no position to alter it. I never asked where stuff came from or who paid for it. I don't remember asking a lot of questions. I do remember telling myself, *Just run the football.*

I was doing what most kids in this situation do and have done. I was getting things my way. Everything was going right. Why shouldn't it? After all, I was different from the other students. It didn't quite make sense but what did I care.

No way was I going to give all of this up. Instead, I would play the game and take things from people who knew no other way than to attach strings and expect returns from boys with bright futures.

Jay saw the coaches moves as straight-up power plays and he didn't like it one bit.

He also wasn't too happy about the fact that I had met a girl. She was a cheerleader and I really liked her.

Tanya came to the varsity field house one day and told Coach Kay that she wanted to meet me. Could he arrange it? The rest was history. But it wasn't like there was anything going on. Tanya and I just talked, went on long walks, went to movies and watched TV. I just liked being with her. Aside from the fact she was a beautiful girl, she was easy to be with. No pressure.

Jay didn't want to hear it. In his mind, girls were trouble. He kept telling everyone involved that he was holding a trump card. He said over and over that he'd play it if he had to.

My relationship
with Tanya, a
Central cheerleader,
never interfered with
my career, although
Uncle Jay didn't
believe it.

14. GHOST

Sometimes I think no matter how old I get I'm never going to shake that ghost that haunts me. I lie awake some nights and ask myself the same questions I've wrestled with for years.

What's my life been so far? What would it feel like to not be haunted? What will happen to me if football doesn't work out? Who will be there to guide me? To show me how to rebuild my life? Who? My ghost? My father.

I know I can't think about it. I have no room for negative thinking. Even less room for failure. I'll make it happen!

Something inside of me commands that I think about my future. Not just what I will achieve, but who I will be. What will make me shine in the spotlight when the uniform and pads are stripped away?

Voices make me doubt myself. I try to blot them out.

When I'm set up deep to return a kickoff, I hear the crowd but I don't actually see the ball being kicked. The football is just a small spinning speck in the sky. My feet know what to do. How to get under it. My eyes are fixed on it, even as an army of men races down the field with the sole thought of taking my head off. Down...down...down...spinning...spinning...spinning Contact! It's on!

The play is "Return Right." All of my blockers and my teammates will be trying their best to make a wall I can use to cut up the right side of the field near the sideline. But by the time I've tucked the football away, there are three guys forcing me to deal with them.

A fake, a juke, a cut, a crossover. Anything to stay on my feet long enough to pick up another block.

Change direction towards the sideline. Return right. Accelerate. Watch my blockers. Use my peripheral vision. Accelerate. Concentrate. Pay no attention to the man in the stands...Grease stained overalls...He's laughing but I can't hear him...Why is he laughing? Concentrate. It's too late. Lights out.

◆◆◆

I talk to my father. I tell him, "I'm not upset with you. I don't blame you. You did what you had to do. Or, what you *wanted* to do. If that's your way, that's your way. I don't understand it, but it's your decision to make. It's not my place to judge you. I can't judge you. I just judge myself."

He never answers. He just laughs and takes a puff off of a dirty old cigar. I can't shake it. It is the ghost of my father.

I don't hate him. I only hate how he haunts me. I fake, juke, cut, side-step. Every time I stand poised for that spinning speck to drop from the sky I think I hear him. But I know better. It ain't him.

15. FLIGHT

SPARKS REPORTEDLY LEAVING CENTRAL HIGH

Derek Sparks, a sophomore running back who rushed for more than 1,394 yards at Central High last fall, will probably enroll at Valley College Prep in San Gabriel on Monday, according to Jay Sparks, his uncle and guardian.

Derek Sparks, who moved from Wharton, Texas to live with his uncle in Long Beach last summer, has not attended Central since the last day of the new semester.

While he said his nephew was happy at Central, Jay Sparks said he wanted to "put him in a more controlled environment. It's important that he gets a solid education," said the elder Sparks.

My head was spinning; it happened so fast. I can't say I was happy about it. But it was true. Jay had made the decision that I would leave Central and enroll in a private school in the San Gabriel Valley.

The newspapers were right; I was happy at Central. Why wouldn't I be happy playing for a powerhouse program in a highly visible league, racking up impressive numbers? Numbers that motivated college recruiters to camp out at Central High School to get a glimpse of my 6-foot, 210-pound frame flying down the field. There was no doubt in my mind that I was living my dream.

Jay told the media that there were two reasons for my abrupt transfer. The first was to give me an opportunity to receive a better education. The second reason was to get me out of a rough neighborhood.

I found out later that there was a much stronger explanation that went deeper than the reasons Jay gave the reporter's.

Months before, on the road, in a game against Crenshaw, who should walk over and shake his hand, but Coach Hutchinson, the former Central head coach who had originally recruited me from Texas.

Hutchinson had his rap all worked out.

He knew all of the things Jay wanted to hear. The right way to question Coach Kay's calls, shaking his head to suggest *that should never be happening.*

Jay was happy to unload his frustrations with the Central program on Hutchinson; and Coach Hutchinson was more than eager to offer his shoulder.

Hutchinson was hungry for a win that day. I was surprised that Jay didn't see it. Or maybe he did. Maybe he just excused it as part of a game everyone was playing.

Jay was hungry for a few things himself. Never mind that the conversation was a violation of by-the-book recruiting regulations. And not just an infraction, but a big time violation.

If it didn't bother Coach Hutchinson, why should it bother Jay? At least, I think that's how he must have felt.

Coach Hutchinson swung into his pitch. He let Jay know that he had landed a position as the assistant head coach at a great little private school in the valley. Valley Prep. Was Jay familiar with it?

"Nah."

"Oh, man it's a great school. I mean, Jay, we're talking about a private school. College preparatory! That's all they do there...get kids ready to be academically competitive in college."

Stop-action on the field. Coach Hutchinson had Jay's full attention.

"It's the kind of program you'd want for Derek," he said. "I mean, the public schools try...but you and I both know what the story is there."

He wasn't completely wrong either. Long Beach schools, as the neighboring Los Angeles Unified School District, was a huge, horribly underfunded, understaffed, and overpopulated system. Whether they wanted to admit to it or not, they had trouble getting quality teachers to work in urban schools. More than that, Central's philosophy seemed to be to keep the kids quiet. Get them in and get them out.

Thirty-nine other students packed most of my classes. If there were more, they'd bring in extra desks and shove us in the room. Because of the huge gang presence, teachers were required to lock all classroom doors. If I decided to head over to the gym instead of hanging in a sardine can of a classroom, who was going to miss me?

Coach Hutchinson hammered Jay with the idea of a private school with a low student-to-teacher ratio. A place that required a hefty tuition to get in. A place suitable for the State Player of the Year.

Then he came at Jay with the *fairness* issue. "After all," Hutchinson argued, "I was the one who arranged for Derek to come to California, not Coach Kay.

"Shoot, Jay," he said with a slap on the back, "that airline ticket came out of my pocket, not his. Now you tell me, does it really seem like Coach Kay appreciates what he's got?

"I read the papers. Everybody sees the lukewarm things he has to say about Derek...

"And what about you? I'll bet Kay hasn't taken advantage of even one of the ideas or connections you brought to the table."

Now, he had Jay's interest.

Hutchinson went in for the kill.

"I mean, look at it this way. It takes the quarterback twisting an ankle to get these guys to give the boy the ball. How many yards and touchdowns would he have by now *if* they were giving him his chances?"

Hutchinson definitely had Jay's attention.

"I'll tell you what." He leaned in. "If they had given the boy the chance we wouldn't be talking right now cause you'd be surrounded by so many college recruiters I wouldn't be able to get to you."

"Coach, I'm not really thinking about recruiters right now," said Jay.

Hutchinson's pitch was slick. "Hey, I understand. All of that will take care of itself.

"By the way, our head coach over at Valley Prep did some coaching over at USC. He and the principal are alumni. They have some pretty good connections there. All of that in its time. The important thing is getting Derek into a program where he can make the most of his opportunities. Get a solid education and mix with, you know, a higher class crowd than what you've got here."

Jay's eyes swept across every section of the crowded Crenshaw stadium stands. Black and brown faces were everywhere.

Hutchinson's speech was hitting home. Besides having Hutchinson's favor, the reason Jay selected Central High over other schools was because it was supposed to be a suburban, not an inner-city school like Crenshaw, Fremont or Washington.

From Jay's viewpoint the environment around Central wasn't much better than an inner-city school. It turned out that the school wasn't nearly as secure as he'd expected.

Now here was a guy offering his nephew a college-prep education in an area far more upscale and safe than in the inner-city.

"Where would Derek stay?" asked Jay.

"Oh, we'll...I mean, we'd work that out," said Hutchinson. "Private schools have a lot more options in arranging that kind of thing.

"Lem'me just tell you this," he confided, "The boosters and supporters of the program will make sure that Derek has the necessities that go along with being a big-time football star. He'll be well taken care of."

Jay's interest was growing intense. He struggled to play it off. "We'll have to think about it," he said.

"Of course," said Hutchinson, "I understand. Listen, take my card and call me when you've given it some more thought. I know you want to watch the game...

"Looks like Derek's gonna tear it up today. I'd just love to see how many yards he could rack up in Valley Prep's league, where the competition isn't as tough. Man oh man," he mused, "it would be like the Derek Sparks League!"

"Yeah, I'll think about it," said Jay, keeping his eyes straight ahead to the field.

"You do that," said Hutchinson smiling. He sensed that he had made inroads.

"I'd love to get you over to see the campus.

"You know, Jay, we could use a man like you out there. I told the principal, who is also the owner of the school, about a couple of those other boys you were trying to bring out here.

"I can't believe that Coach Kay threw away the chance to get them out here. If I put you together with my boss I believe you could become the *Texas Connection*. Keep in touch."

The *Texas Connection*. Jay loved the notion of it on many levels. It felt good to hear Coach Hutchinson tell him that he could be of value, that his contributions would be appreciated. He might even make a name for himself. *The Texas Connection was Jay's life dream.*

Jay knew so many talented young men in Texas who would never get the publicity they needed to attract a college scholarship. Jay also felt that the atmosphere at Central wasn't right for me, or kids like me. If he could bring enough kids out to California, he could even set up the *Texas Connection Home.*

The *home* could have someone (like him) watching over all these gifted kids, helping them make the most of their athletic talents and ensuring that they earn their diplomas. For the first time, Jay was seeing his idea progress towards a real possibility.

He had been talking to my mom and their sister back in Texas. They were not happy about the Long Beach neighborhood I was living in, nor with the fact that I was living on my own.

Jay was also concerned that living in Wharton, Preston's exposure and chances of being recruited by major universities were slim. He felt that with my success, Preston would grow depressed if he didn't get out of Wharton. His grades would drop. California would be good for him as a student-athlete. But Preston's mom sure didn't want to send him to California to live in an apartment somewhere in a city surrounded by gang activity.

◆◆◆

Right after the season ended at Central, Jay showed up at my door.

"We got to talk."

"Come on in," I said. I was watching TV with Tanya, my girlfriend. Tanya and I were getting closer and closer. Jay stared at her for a long time.

"Would you excuse us?" The look on his face was all she needed to see that Jay wasn't playing around. And I knew better than to say anything. So I just nodded to her as she gathered up her books and left.

Jay looked around at the apartment. I had always been big on neatness, so at least the place looked presentable. But it could have been the Taj Mahal, and Jay wouldn't have been happy.

"So you're a grown man, huh?" He was standing with his hands on his hips, even though I was still sitting comfortably on the couch.

"Uncle Jay, nothing was going on."

"When I brought you out here, D, I told you there were three rules: No turning back, do your school work, and no girls. But you're making your own rules now aren't you?"

"No," I protested.

"Looks to me like you are. Looks to me like you're living up in here like you think you're in charge. You got nobody to answer to. Now, all of a sudden, you don't have to listen to the things I say."

"I do listen, Jay. I got an adult living with me."

"Don't you try to run that game on me, boy. You may think you know it all, but I know a thing or two myself. These coaches have you believing their line of bull so much you're full of it yourself.

"I'm talking about having somebody look out for you who cares what happens to you five, ten, years from now. Not some hired yes man who'll squat down and kiss your backside just to get you to run touchdowns.

"You made an agreement with me and now you stand up in here acting like it ain't no big deal."

"I'm not doing that."

"What do you think it means when I say NO GIRLS? You think it means sitting here on the couch alone with one? Together? When you got books over there on the shelf that have been there so long that they're collecting dust?"

"No, Uncle Jay. I don't think that. I'm sorry."

"You're not near as sorry as you'll be if you look up one day and your chance to be somebody has slipped by while you were kissing on that girl. When that day comes you're going to realize that you don't have enough education to fill out a job application."

"I'm sorry, Jay. I like her. She's the only person I can talk to."

Jay didn't speak but I could see that he wasn't angry anymore. I guess he knew what it's like to be lonely and on your own. He sat down next to me on the couch.

"I think it's time we made a move away from Central."

"Jay, I said I'm sorry!"

"This has nothing to do with all of that." He waved the air dismissively. "This is about a better opportunity."

"What could be a better opportunity than playing for Central?"

Jay unloaded the whole story of Valley Prep, the kind of school it was and what it had to offer.

"You think it's better for me to go from a top rated 4-A team to a Single-A school nobody ever heard of?"

"The less competition you have, the more touchdowns you score. It's not like the school is in Bakersfield or somewhere. Besides, the more recognition you get now, the more colleges will come calling."

"But the coaches at Central have already planned the season around me."

"Like they planned it around Keith Walker last year?" Jay shouted.

"He got hurt."

"Oh, and you're Superman. You'll never get hurt?"

He was making sense, but I didn't know if I was ready to just pick up and leave. It didn't seem right. "Don't I owe an explanation to the team?"

"What do you owe them."

"What do I owe?" In my mind, Jay's rhetorical question was ridiculous. "Look around the apartment, Jay. Read the newspapers."

"I'm talking about getting you into a school that most kids pay a lot of money to attend. Top quality teachers and classes where you can actually learn something instead of sitting around reading your clippings in the papers. I talked to your mama, and she thinks this is the best thing." Now he was pulling out the heavy artillery.

"But she's never seen Central," I said.

"You wanna call her up and tell her that?"

Right. I knew there was no point in that. Mom didn't like me arguing with her, whether I was in her house or not.

At this point the biggest thing on my mind, I have to admit, was Tanya. I could play football anywhere. It wasn't like I was so in love with Central, but this was my first time in any kind of a relationship and I didn't want to leave it behind. It crossed my mind that Jay had been right when he said girls would be a distraction.

He must have been telepathic that day. "You've got plenty of time to be with girls. Now is the only time you're gonna have to get yourself into a top college. The head coach at Valley Prep is hooked in with the coaches at USC."

"For real?" Now he had my attention.

"For real!" He looked up at me out of the corner of his eye, like he wanted to see if I was ready for what he had to say next. Then he laid the big news on me.

"And if things go the way I expect, your cousin Preston will be out here playing with you."

"No way!" I couldn't help but grin. I wished for my cousin's success as much as my own and I missed him. Still there was Tanya.

"Why doesn't Preston just go to Valley Prep and play there, and I'll stay at Central?" That way, I reasoned, I could see Preston *and* Tanya.

He looked solemnly towards the wall. "They won't take him without you."

◆◆◆

A few days later I had a strange feeling as I walked around the apartment packing up my stuff. I had acquired a few more things since arriving from Wharton, but I still didn't have much. Tanya was with me. We spent the day crying, packing a little, and crying some more.

I tried to think of good things to say, or ways to make it seem that we could still be together somehow. But we both knew that once I walked out of the door there'd be no looking back. My coaches, my uncle, and even my own commitment would see to that. This was good-bye and we both knew it.

I thought about whether I should go to Central's football office and say something to the coaches. They had treated me well and had given me the opportunity to prove myself. But when I thought about it, there wasn't much I could say. I figured they knew better than I did that those were the breaks of the game.

Did that make it right? Probably not.

As I exited the apartment, I took one last glance and closed the door.

I walked Tanya to the corner without knowing how to say good-bye. Words had never been my thing. The best I could do was give her a hug and say..."See ya."

"Yeah," she said quietly, "see ya."

I turned and walked away, not wanting to drag this out. I walked fast but I couldn't help stopping to take a last look at her. Tanya was smiling. She flashed me a "V" for victory, the sign the cheerleaders gave as we took the field. I waved my No. 1 sign. And I moved on to Valley Prep.

16. Valley Prep

Once Jay made his decision I thought I was ready.

I was wrong.

I had always held an image of the San Gabriel Valley as this really neat, clean place with sprawling lawns, nice cars and people walking up to you with their morning papers, asking, "How are you doing today?"

My vision of a college preparatory school was like an old-time movie, where the teacher walks around in a robe, clutching a thickly bound book of classic literature against his chest. Something straight out of *The Dead Poets Society*. I saw myself strolling through the gardens, past a poetry reading held in the shade of a beautiful Spanish fountain.

Wrong!

Valley Prep was the tiniest school I had ever seen. There were no towers or spacious lawns. The place looked like a tool shed. When I first saw it, I thought I was at a Motel 6!

I learned later it was exactly that. A converted motel. And the town, where the school was located, didn't look a whole lot different from the neighborhood surrounding Long Beach's Central High.

If they had promised me a better education, they must have meant that it was in Socio-Economics. At the entrance of the school there were real live prostitutes. I could not believe my senses. My mouth was wide open, my ears were pinned back and my eyes were glued to the fishnets and knee-high boots the hookers were wearing. One had enough make-up on to put Max Factor to shame. What was going on?

At first I thought it was some kind of joke, an initiation of some sort. But I quickly saw otherwise. I had heard of hole-in-the-wall places, but here I couldn't see the wall for all the holes! It scared me.

I took a close look at Jay to see if maybe he hadn't gone a little crazy. He patted me reassuringly.

The scenario was surreal. A demented Disneyland.

The classes were all held in a two-story motel structure just beyond the parking lot. Every slot on the lot was occupied by expensive cars—like new BMWs, Mercedes coups and every kind of sports car I had ever seen in magazines. It was obvious that the students at Valley Prep came from wealthy families. I couldn't believe parents with so much money sent their kids to a dump like this.

Central High was looking better and better with every moment I spent at Valley Prep. I didn't know whether to scream, cry or try to kill Jay.

My next great surprise came when I discovered that the school didn't have a football stadium. Now I was really tripping.

My uncle had pulled me out of a school where I played for the City 4-A Championship in the L.A. Coliseum, to come to a Motel 6, without a football stadium in the worst part of the Valley! And hookers!

Two coaches came out to greet us. I had nothing to say to anybody. It was going to be the toughest sell they had ever made. I didn't know that *sell* was these guys' middle name. They knew their stuff. If those two coaches had been in the real estate business, Donald Trump would have something to worry about.

The assistant, Coach Hutchinson, was an affable outgoing guy. He slapped me on the back and went into his sales pitch. "It's about time we got you out here where you belong!"

He was the first to call me back in Texas while I was still in the ninth grade. We had had several conversations.

I thought back to the day at school when I told Omar, "Come over to my house after school. There's this coach from California who's gonna call today and talk to us about playing for him at some big school in Los Angeles."

Neither Omar nor I knew exactly what that meant, but we were excited the whole day. When the final class bell rang, we sprinted all the way home.

Coach Hutchinson talked a long time with both of us, telling us how great it was to play football in Los Angeles. Ending the call, he reminded us that our phone conversations should stay between us. We hung up and jumped around the room like we had just won the lottery.

Now, standing on the Valley Prep campus, Coach Hutchinson was ready to pick up where he left off. He began by introducing the head coach, J.K. Santini. Santini was beaming. He chuckled to himself as he shook my hand.

They had their whole show worked out. Talk about a difference from my first day at Central!

The coaches at Valley Prep didn't waste any time making me feel like I was their top priority, showing how happy they were to have me visit their school. It was the smart thing to do because it put me at ease and made me feel better about the move.

They also made it a point to acknowledge Jay, calling him by his first name and including him in the conversation.

The way he was nodding and smiling, it looked to me like Jay was already sold on this place. That made me angry. I kept quiet, though, and listened to what the coaches had to say.

"Derek, a player like you needs a quality program and a staff who can introduce you to the *right* people, said Coach Hutchinson. "With you carrying the ball for Valley Prep, we know we're going to win the CIF championship."

He paused to see if he had my full attention. "But we need to think beyond that. We need to begin considering which college will be the best for you to play for. Where you'll get the most exposure, so that when you sign your NFL contract you'll go to the best team and sign for the most money."

They talked about my future like it was a foregone conclusion. Like it was a done deal and I was ready to sign a professional contract. It was weird. There I was, 15-years-old, listening to a couple of strangers talk about how many millions I was going to make. But as they built their fantasy, I had to confess that their speech had whet my appetite.

They gave us a tour of the campus, careful to begin with the library and a few of the classrooms. They were by far the most impressive thing I'd seen so far. Inside one of those crummy looking motel rooms was a fantastic library stocked, floor to ceiling, with books. Every classroom contained a horde of state-of-the-art computer equipment.

At Central, students spilled out of the classrooms and into the grafitti strewn halls. At Valley Prep there were plenty of empty seats in each class. The coaches laid it on thick about the quality of education at Valley Prep. How this school prepared their students to handle the academic rigors of any university.

They had Jay drooling. They snagged my attention by dropping names of all the coaches and players they knew at USC and UCLA. How they had coached players who were attending big schools on athletic scholarships. They went on about the widespread notoriety these players were enjoying and how the college recruiters were lining up to get a look the new crop of talent at Valley Prep. College recruiters appreciated knowing that their athletes maintained a solid grade point average. It made their jobs easier.

Jay gave me a sideways glance. It was the same rap he himself had been preaching for years and he wanted to be sure it was sinking in. I was still a long way from being sold, though. To my way of thinking, things were working out just fine at Central.

"Where's the football stadium?" I asked, hiding my contempt, knowing that there was no stadium.

Coach Hutchinson pounced on the question. "Oh, we don't play here on campus. Our games are mostly played on a college field. It's an incredible college stadium that seats nearly twice as many fans as your old school. And we fill those seats up every single game. We hold night games, under the lights, with a professional p.a. system so sweet it sounds like the Super Bowl when they announce your name."

He cupped his hands over his mouth, "Starting at running back...number 35...Derek...Sparks!"

Hearing my name lightened my spirits. The guy had done his homework. He knew what was important to me. He knew my jersey number!

Santini, Hutchinson and Uncle Jay moved me quickly to the gymnasium. An amazing building, the kind you'd expect to see in Beverly Hills High.

All of the equipment was brand new. Just stepping onto the newly waxed hardwood of the basketball court was exciting. If I had been a basketball player I might have been sold. But I was here to play football.

Coach Santini took his cue from Coach Hutchinson. He was a powerful looking man, although not especially tall or wide. His power was in his eyes. Dark and piercing, with thick bushy brows, Coach Santini never took his eyes off of me. He had chosen not to say much up to this point, and now he spoke with the confidence of a man who had been around the block.

"Derek...Jay, let's step over to our football team's practice facility. I think you'll find that what we don't have on campus here in terms of a stadium, we make up for in the quality of our training complex."

He couldn't have been more right. Their workout field was tiny, but stocked with everything a player needed. Tackling dummies, blocking pads, sleds. You name it. The weight room looked like they were expecting Arnold Schwarzenegger. It was impressive.

Coach Santini turned up the heat.

"The problem with public schools is they don't have enough funds to properly train an athlete of your caliber." *Those eyes.*

"And what little money they do have, they mishandle."

"Here," he gestured majestically at the room but never took his gaze off of me, "here money is no object."

Looking around the room it appeared that he was right. I was speechless. Jay was grinning.

Coach Hutchinson jumped back in. "Let's go take a look at where you'll be living."

They walked us over to another part of campus, behind the motel, where I expected to find some type of dormitory-style boarding facility. Instead, they showed me a four bedroom house.

"I think you'll find this to be exactly what we discussed, Jay." I was dumb struck.

Coach Hutchinson added with a smirk, "Plenty of room. Nice and quiet. All fenced in so Derek can concentrate on his studies, and right here on campus where there are no distractions."

I spoke up. "It'll be just me living here?"

"For the most part," said Hutchinson. I thought he was a little nervous.

"We might move a couple of other players in just to keep you company," the coach said, waving and pointing out all the amenities.

Then he added for Jay's benefit, "Of course we'll have to work out the right adult supervision. I don't think that's going be a problem."

The coaches concluded everything with chuckles, back slaps and hand shakes. I wasn't too fond of the constant smirking and winking occurring between them.

"How does that work?" I asked out of nowhere.

"How does what work, son?" Coach Santini was smiling.

"How can I be living on campus when all the other students don't?"

Coach Santini flashed me what he considered a reassuring smile.

"Valley Prep is a licensed boarding facility. We don't often have the need to offer housing, but every now and then, in a special case like yours, we can make it happen."

"That's the beauty of it!" Coach Hutchinson volunteered.

I was still not convinced.

"But won't the media and the CIF Southern Section give me trouble about that?"

For the first time the coaches dropped their jovial smiles and looked at me seriously. Coach Santini did the talking.

"Son," he said, gripping my arm powerfully, "you just run the football, and let us worry about all of the other stuff."

There it was again. *Just run the football.*

"Yeah," I said. "Okay. I just figured..."

The head coach took Uncle Jay off to discuss the fine details of *the deal.* Coach Hutchinson led me on the rest of the tour. He knew what he was doing and his timing was perfect.

We walked across the campus as the lunch bell rang and students poured out of the unusual looking classrooms. I had never seen so many good looking girls in one place in my life!

One after another, the coach pulled the best looking girls aside to introduce me. He always started by saying, "Derek is the Sophomore State Player of the Year. He'll be transferring to Valley Prep and playing a little football in the spring."

The girls seemed pleased. A couple of them giggled but most were more sophisticated. "It's a pleasure meeting you," they said, offering me one manicured hand after another. I lost count of how many beautiful girls I met in those few minutes.

Coach Hutchinson suggested that I get some lunch while he finished talking with Jay and the head coach. He pressed some Valley Prep hospitality into my palm, and waved over a pretty blonde who escorted me to the lunch facility. As I paid for lunch I realized that what he gave me was a lot more than I needed.

Just run the football. The subject was closed.

17. TANDEM

The coaches had failed to mention a few things during our tour. Their most important omission was Marcus Wright-Fair.

At Central, I had never paid much attention to the WAC League or to Valley Prep. Marcus Wright-Fair was a returning senior for Valley Prep, a tailback who had rushed for 1,519 yards the previous season. That's 25 yards more than I had gained at Central; and I led the Southern Pacific League, as well as the city, in rushing.

He was a player accustomed to carrying the ball 25 to 30 times a game, not leaving many carries for another running back. It also meant the star in a lot of people's minds was Marcus Wright-Fair, including Marcus's. He had been at Valley Prep since junior high and had paid his dues. It seemed to me that he was all the running back a team like Valley Prep needed.

It seemed clear why no one had mentioned Marcus. They knew that it would make me uneasy. I began to wonder why I was really there.

From what I later read, they had told Marcus that they were bringing in a blocking fullback, but not a running back of comparable ability.

I also discovered that most of the information distributed to the players was on a need-to-know basis. They told us just enough to make us give them our best efforts.

All questions got answered in the same way. "Don't worry, we'll take care of it. Just run the ball."

I wasn't thrilled to learn about Marcus. And I could only imagine how Marcus must have felt about me. How could he see me as anything but a threat? How could this situation be anything but tense?

Then I picked up the Valley edition of the *Los Angeles Times,* and my speculations were confirmed. The reporter asked Coach Santini which of his running backs would be carrying the ball:

> *Fortunately for Coach J.K. Santini, he doesn't have to choose between the two. Sparks is a fullback.*
>
> *"Wright-Fair is my tailback and primary ball carrier and that stays," Santini said. They'll be on the field at the same time. They'll be complementing each other. I've made it clear to them they won't be competing against each other."*

I was nervous about meeting Marcus and I wasn't sure what I would say to him. But when the moment came, and we met face to face, Marcus and I hit it off immediately.

Marcus was a great person and he showed instant respect for my numbers. Just as I did his. We simply decided to make the best of the predicament, and it showed. The media followed:

> *Wright-Fair is 6-2, 205-pounds and quick. He runs hard, in an upright manner, conjuring images of NFL star, Eric Dickerson.*
>
> *As a junior last season, he rushed for 1,519 yards and scored 17 touchdowns. He carried the ball 7.2 yards every time he touched it.*
>
> *Recruiters from USC, UCLA, West Virginia, Miami, and Oklahoma State were camping out on his lawn.*
>
> *The WAC League, most thought at the end of last year, would be his own little romping ground for even grander days this season...*
>
> *All of a sudden, he was faced with the prospect of, gulp, sharing the ball. Strangely, he couldn't be happier.*
>
> *Because in Sparks, Wright-Fair has a good friend. And vice versa.*
>
> *It all goes back to that day when they first met. Wright-Fair treated Sparks to lunch. With a hamburger and some pieces of chicken between them, it was the beginning of a friendship.*

> *"I go by the house, we go out to movies, we go out with girls," Wright-Fair said. "We hit it off like friends. Just friends."*
>
> *"We've grown pretty close," Sparks said. "He comes to my house. We sit and talk. We go out. He helps me out. Whenever I need anything he says, 'Hey, give me a call or tell me. I'll help you out.'"*
>
> *Said Wright-Fair, "We have never had a fight to this day, grudges, arguments or anything like that."*

Even as I read it today, it sounds like were well rehearsed. And we were. Granted, we were friendly, but it wasn't like we were brothers.

It's just that after so many years of having sports writers attempt to trip us up, we had both learned how to handle the media. In the coming months we got better and better at it.

> *"Look, I haven't sat up saying, If Marcus gets the ball so many times a game, what do I have left?" Sparks said. "The way I look at it is, if we run '24 Power' five times in a row and the defense is pulling to Marcus, let's trick the defense once and give it to me.*
>
> *"He can get five carries to my one, as long as it helps the team win."*

Yeah, right. I can't imagine any running back who would be happy with that, let alone California's State Sophomore Player of the Year. But even then, I knew what had to be said.

> *"As long as we get to that final game and get the jackets, the rings, the trophy and the publicity."*

Then, to the heart of the matter...

> *Wright-Fair and Sparks have formed a power alliance in pursuit of the common goal, the CIF Southern Section Championship.*
>
> *"Let's put it this way," Wright-Fair said, "anytime I get the ball, I'm trying to go for six. I'm not going to think, 'Oh I'll never get that many times to carry the ball, he's going to get all the carries.' I'm not going to put it that way. I'm going to make it count every time. That's the way I look at it."*

It sounded good on paper, but I didn't see any way a running back of Marcus's caliber could be that casual about how many carries he's given.

Especially because he was a senior, Marcus was well aware that college recruiters were salivating in the stands.

> If four carries a game will win, I'll do it," Sparks said. "But if I get the ball only four times a game, I'm going to try to get four touchdowns. I'm going to make something of it."

I'm proud to say, I never did have any personal problems with Marcus and I think he felt the same about me. But neither of us was happy about the way the coaches had spun the situation; using us, telling each of us precisely what we wanted to hear. They had ultimately and willfully created a competition between us. It was their control device, a strategy I saw used by coaches throughout my intercollegiate career.

To tell the truth, coaches never had a problem with a little competition because they benefited greatly from us running up the score board.

◆◆◆

One more thing neither Jay nor the coaches had mentioned was the deal they had struck regarding my living arrangements.

Uncle Jay, who was concerned about my supervision, was, at the same time, worried about his brother, my Uncle Tom, who was living somewhere in the South and not doing well. He didn't have the means to bring Tom into his carpet cleaning business, so Jay had been trying to get Tom back on his feet and into a solid career.

The coaches at Valley Prep proposed a solution to alleviate both of Jay's problems at the same time.

Valley Prep would arrange for Tom to come out to California where he would become a member of the staff as the boarding school supervisor. Boarding School Supervisor? There was only one actual boarder on the entire campus. Me!

Nevertheless Tom would draw a salary as boarding school supervisor and live in the house on campus with me. Then, to give him greater responsibility, my cousin Preston, who had distinguished himself as a receiver back in Wharton, would come out and join us at Valley Prep. It had all been arranged.

Tom would have a job and a place to stay rent free. He'd also be paid for his secondary positions as "campus caretaker" and "assistant football coach."

I never saw him do much caretaking aside from making sure that Preston and I got to practice on time. Despite Tom's lack of coaching experience, Tom was one of the highest paid assistant coaches in California. And he'd be right there to report any suspicious dealings to Jay.

Jay said that Tom's presence would guarantee that Preston and I were being accommodated. That was Jay's way of making sure that the Valley Prep coaches lived up to their promises.

How did I feel about all of this? The house, the money, the deals? At that point, it was all fine with me. Everyone was benefiting. I had some nagging feelings but I left them at that. I was there to run the football. Everything else was being taken care of.

18. THE HOUSE

Preston's arrival at Valley Prep was the best thing that could have happened to me. His presence helped me to relax about the growing controversy surrounding my transfer.

Preston hadn't changed a bit. He was wild, but he also had the same quiet disposition I had. When the two of us were together, we talked and laugh for hours and hours. Or, we could be in the same room saying nothing.

Preston was pumped about being in California. I knew some of it was just plain relief to finally be out of Wharton. For him, L.A. was a combination of escape, adventure and reunion.

With Tom as our supervisor, Jay dropped by as often as he could. It wasn't like Texas, but I was satisfied to have some of my family members in California, and it felt good. It wasn't long before I pushed all thoughts of Central out of my mind.

Preston, who was one of the best all-around athletes I had ever known, was excited about playing for Valley Prep. He went on and on about how he was going to rewrite the record book. How he was going to rule the league in receptions and touchdowns. He was going to total more yards than anyone ever had at that position.

I was happy to see him so excited, but I wondered too how he was going to total all those yards on a team with a reputation for never throwing the ball; a team with two 1500-yard running backs, no quarterback I had ever heard of.

Preston continued spouting off. He bragged about what the coaches told him. What they had promised him. Then I knew. They had given him the same "star of our team" speech I'd received on my first day.

Preston was convinced that the team was being built around him, just as I had been. I didn't tell him about Marcus Wright-Fair. I figured he'd find out soon enough. The way I saw it, we were all in for some surprises.

In the next few days two other players, Leon Lett and John Pearlman, moved into the house on campus. Leon was a huge black lineman raised in Arkansas. He was a Southern boy like Preston and me.

Leon said he had no idea how Valley Prep got a hold of his video footage. Within a couple of months, though, he said, he and his family relocated to Los Angeles and he was enrolled at Valley Prep.

I wondered if the move had anything to do with Leon's talents as a sturdy 6-foot-7, 300-pound lineman, who blew his opponents off the line of scrimmage. It didn't take a genius to figure out why he was here.

Leon told me confidentially that he figured highly into the coaches' plans for this year. He was going to be the man. At least that's what they promised him.

From the beginning, I wasn't too thrilled to share a house with Leon. The boy was a mess! Leon left everything dirty, including himself, and was allergic to any kind of housework.

You'd think he would have been appreciative to be living in a nice house, with his own room in the San Gabriel Valley.

Foul odors, seeping from Leon's bedroom, waged war with my nose. We'd force him to close the door, just to keep the smell from spreading to the rest of the house. I didn't even want to think about what could make the room smell that bad. He was simply one nasty boy.

But, oh, could Leon play football. He was perfect for opening holes in the defensive line, and this made him a running backs dream. He was a good kid. I liked him; I just hated his mess.

John Pearlman, our other surprise roommate, was altogether another story. Fair and lanky, with dancing eyes, John's manner was totally gregarious and there seemed to be nothing in this world he was afraid of.

I had never met a wild white guy before and I didn't want to know what he was into. I was, however, curious about what the coaches had promised

John to get him to Valley Prep.

He boasted about his future as the greatest linebacker in Valley Prep history, but compared to the competition, John was a bean-pole. How was he going to stand up in the middle of our defense at his size?

John had only played "B" football at Grant Hills High the year before. He said that he'd done well, but I didn't see how that could count for anything at the varsity level.

By now I figured the coaches were promising their players, and whoever else they were trying to sway, anything they wanted to hear. Or thought they wanted to hear.

I wanted to find out what John's deal was, but I couldn't get him to slow down long enough to ask him. John Pearlman was a talker! And people couldn't get enough of it. John had charisma.

When I finally got to ask him how he ended up at Valley Prep, I got a real education.

John had dropped by Valley Prep one day to hit on a girl who went there and bumped into Coach Hutchinson. Hutchinson, the consummate recruiter, recognized John and asked him if he was happy at Grant Hills.

"Yeah, I'm happy enough," John said. John had a way of staying happy about things.

Hutchinson went into his pitch. "Seems to me you wouldn't be so happy playing on the "B" team when you could be starting varsity."

"I don't really have the size, you know?" John said.

Hutchinson's eyes narrowed. "Well, if you were in the right program, that kind of stuff could be taken care of.

"What are you doing with yourself in the off season?"

John's mood sagged a little. "Well, I should be playing baseball, but I'm, uh, ineligible right now, you know...academically." This stung. John's real talent was on the baseball field.

Hutchinson smiled and put his arm around John. "What if you were going to a school where that could be taken care of?"

"Taken care of?" asked John.

"You come here, we can have those grades changed. You'll be on the baseball field in a couple of days."

"I can't afford to come to this place," said John.

"Who said anything about paying? I'm telling you, you do what we tell you, and we'll take care of all of the little problems. Give it some thought."

John jumped. "I don't have to think about it. It's on!" Like I said, John was a wild guy.

Just like that, it was a done deal.

John transferred that week and in no time he was known throughout the campus. That's the kind of guy he was. He went after what he wanted, and aside from girls, what John wanted most was to play baseball.

This happened overnight too. His grade point average soared past the minimum requirement within a matter of hours.

His age jumped backwards as well. John was in the second semester of his junior year at Grant Hills, which would only make him eligible to play football for one season at Valley Prep. So when he arrived at Valley Prep, he became a sophomore. It was all taken care of.

John and Preston played baseball together, and they tore it up both on and off the field. Preston was the starting center fielder and an instant star of the team. John was right behind him. In his first day at practice John cranked three home runs and was the man to beat in left field.

John was also a ladies man. That's probably why he and Preston hit it off immediately. Preston had always liked the girls. But in this department, he had nothing on John.

I'm pretty sure that John would have stayed with baseball and blown off football completely if things had gone his way. But they didn't. John's mouth and appetite for women proved to be his downfall.

It hadn't taken John much time at all to become tight with the guys on the baseball team. It took even less time for him to make sure the best look-ing girls on campus knew him personally.

He had set his sights on Gina, a girl who had as much sex appeal as her parents had money. And let me tell you, that was a lot.

As with most things John went after, it didn't take long for them to hook up. Soon after, John paid his first all night visit to the guest house of her parents mansion.

The next day at practice Preston teased John during the team stretch.

"Yo, Johnee-John. Why do you need to stretch, when you told me you spent the whole night stretching it out?"

John took the bait. "Well, I stretched her out...but I was kinda stiff all night long. You know what I'm saying?" The players and coaches hooted and hollered.

"Is the rich young thang as good as what you used to get on the other side of the hills?" Preston goaded.

"Let me tell you something. Don't believe that bull you hear about rich girls being uptight. They are freaks! I thought I died and went to heaven."

Some of the other players joined the tease about John's prowess. "Did you knock them boots, Jonnnnny?"

And John went into full swing. "As soon as she can walk again why don't you get her out here and ask her?"

"Oooohhhhh!" the players cackled.

A couple of the coaches pretended to sneeze into their fists. "Bull" they sneezed! The team busted up.

"For real!" John protested. "I tore it up. I put in work. I mean overtime! Rich girls must bathe in milk cause she was as smooth as whipped cream! And when I gave her a taste of 'Johnny-John' the rest was history."

Now everybody was a part of the act, laughing and throwing in lewd comments. The coaches even joined in the laughter. John bragged some more.

"I'm kinda scared to go to class today, cause I know she'll be in there crying my name. 'Johnny, Johnny.'"

"She goes here?" asked one of the players. Now the whole team was really curious.

"Oh, yeah," said John. "I don't mess around. She's only the finest thing in this school. You know, that fine fox, Gina? The one who drives that red 450 SL?"

The players went crazy. Everybody agreed that she was of the best looking girls at Valley Prep.

All of a sudden one of the coaches barked at the team, "That's enough screwing around!"

The players went through an unusually grueling workout. At the end, when the coach announced the starting lineup for the next scrimmage, the players were surprised to hear John was not among them.

John asked why he'd been left out of the lineup. He was told, "Players don't question coaches' decisions."

The next day, John was holding court in the parking lot. Gina confronted him in tears.

"I can't believe you! Why'd you go telling everybody that you made it with me?"

John, surrounded by players and other students, was not the type to lose face in front of anybody. "I did, didn't I?"

"And you announced it to the whole baseball team! You're such a loser!"

John wondered which of his teammates had run to her and sold him out, but he played it cool.

"And you're easy! So get out of my face."

Gina ran off crying. Even though John had saved face he felt bad about the way he had treated her. Underneath his outward, flashy wild-man style and teenage macho strutting, John was actually a sensitive guy with a good heart.

That night he went to Gina's house to apologize, and Gina was happy to accept. She was also happy to accept John's company in her huge mansion one more time.

As John was leaving in the early morning hours, he promised not to talk anymore in front of the team. Gina looked at him sadly.

"You'll be lucky if you're playing baseball."

John felt confused, and wanted to know what she meant.

Gina shook her head softly and ran her fingers through John's blonde hair. "Oh Johnny, didn't you know? I've been making it with your coach since I was a sophomore."

John never got close to the starting lineup again. Not even close.

Knowing that he had stepped in it pretty bad, he went to the coach to try to talk it out. A married man, the coach had nothing to say on the matter until John was leaving. Then the coach offered a parting statement. "You're playing days on this team are done, stud. You'll never see the field."

John was in shock. Baseball was his life. It was the reason he had transferred to Valley Prep in the first place. Now, he knew his big mouth had all but erased that dream.

He ran straight to the football office to talk to Coach Hutchinson, who had recruited him in the first place.

"Coach Miller is screwing me out of playing because I bagged his mistress."

Coach Hutchinson chuckled. "Damn, I though you were smarter than that, kid!"

John was near tears. "This is serious, man. I should be on that field in the starting lineup! You gotta help me!"

"What for? Why do you want to waste your time playing baseball anyway? You need to get your mind on football, kid. This is going to be a championship football team, and you could be the guy that makes it happen. I'm gonna make you the star of the greatest high school football team this state has ever seen. There'll be so many recruiters out here, waving scholarships in your face, you won't be able to see straight.

"Don't you want to win the CIF Southern Section championship, and be living like a king?"

He had John's full attention.

"Sure, but what college is gonna recruit me?"

"Try USC, or UCLA, for starters. You name it. They're not gonna even notice you if you waste the entire spring lookin' like a skinny faggot for baseball, when we could be bulking you up to the size to kick butt in the Pac-10."

"You think I should juice up, coach?"

He was talking about steroids, illegal on every level of athletics, not to mention their dangerous side effects.

"Get out of here, you puss. I thought you were tough. I thought you had some brains. You're not even smart enough to spell greatness. Go cry to Coach Miller and suck up to him. Maybe he'll let you be the batboy for their games.

"If you want to be something special on the football field, then you come back and talk to me."

John didn't eat dinner that night. We tried to get him to talk about it, but he wanted to be alone. He just locked himself up in his room and cried all night. Finally, when the sun rose, John decided to become the greatest linebacker Valley Prep had ever seen. He went back to Hutchinson's office, and a few days later, he had his first appointment with the steroid doctor.

19. REALITY

Did I see it? Did I know the new world I was living in was a dangerous, unwholesome place? I saw it, but I didn't want to acknowledge it.

I was enrolled in a school where the officials didn't think twice about violating any regulation standing between them and the recruitment of an attractive prospect. They didn't give a hang about the players. We were nothing more than prospects and recruits. We were the commodity.

Money was no object, as the coaches were happy to demonstrate. Any given day I could go by the office and say, "Coach, I need some sweats."

At Central, somehow it would be arranged and I would have my sweats. But at Valley Prep, the coaches reached into their pockets and handed over whatever cash they had. No questions asked.

If they didn't have enough to cover it, they'd tell me to hold on. Fifteen minutes later, they'd always come back with more money.

This all occurred with the blessing of the school's principal and owner, Pop Wilson. Pop was a powerful man who wanted championships and media exposure, at all costs.

As for me, if someone wanted to put a hundred dollar bill in my hand, I was okay with it.

Did I know I was at a school where the truth was swept under the rug? A school built on illegalities? I knew it. But the Valley Prep machine had the power and the throttle was open. The machine kept moving full steam ahead. I was just one of its working parts.

Every day one of the coaches or administrators assured me that Valley Prep's methods were no different than other schools. This was the way it was done for exceptional athletes. I figured they knew and I trusted them to be right.

Besides, I was brought here by the man I trusted most, to live with my cousin and my uncle. My family wouldn't steer me the wrong way. Day in and day out, my teenage brain was programmed and reprogrammed by the hype.

My focus was on my mission to become a football star. I was preoccupied with earning a scholarship to UCLA or USC and moving on to the NFL.

Did I know about the steroids? Did I know that the coaches encouraged players to use them? I didn't want to know, so I shut it out and pretended I didn't.

Did I understand that I was in a high school where special allowances for star athletes were the rule and not the exception? Where coaches flirt and sleep with students as part of the norm? I knew all right. But I didn't care. I just ran the football.

What my mind was not on, was school. I had arrived at the beginning of the spring semester, the off-season for football. The coaches told me to concentrate on getting in better shape, learn the Valley Prep offense, and bond with my teammates. That was my job. Classes were not.

I never had to go to class. I went if I felt like it, and if class didn't get in the way of football.

If I didn't like a class, the coaches would say, "Well Derek, come on in here and watch a film. Learn the playbook."

More often than not, that's what I would do. My grades just got taken care of.

What 16-year-old do you know, who would go to class when he could get a "B" just hanging around the football department?

I'm not saying I never went to class. Down deep, it nagged at me, but there were plenty of days when I just didn't feel like going. I completed my homework on time, but I never felt any pressure to learn.

I knew that Jay would be unhappy if he knew about my studies, but he didn't know because he wasn't there. Valley Prep was more than 30 freeway miles from Inglewood, where Jay lived, and he was having a tough time balancing work with his new marriage.

Jay knew that he wouldn't have any time to look after Preston and me.

That was the reason he had brought his brother, Tom, to Valley Prep.

But Tom...Tom was not Jay. I loved Tom. He had the biggest heart in the world and was the most loyal person you'd ever want to meet, especially with his family. At least back then he was.

If anyone in our family had a problem, Tom dropped what he was doing and settled the matter. Tom's way of settling things tended to be extreme. He was often irrational.

When he lived in Texas, Tom lived hard, partied hard and stayed in trouble with the law. It wasn't unusual to see him packing a gun on any occasion. A gun he wasn't afraid to use.

I thought everything about Tom was cool. He had a cool swaggering walk and a cool way of talking. Tom wore dark glasses, day and night.

At 6-3, 280-pounds, he was never the guy to mess with and he didn't take any lip. Still, he could always make people laugh, and if he cared about you, he'd do almost anything to help you.

Tom was never the ideal choice to supervise Preston and me. Or to make sure that we got an education. Tom liked to have too much fun. And there was always a reason to party. If someone had a little something to smoke or to drink, Tom was down with that.

The huge den in the house became his bedroom. We all knew better than to go in there. Tom would be off in there drinking his "Seven and Sevens," entertaining ladies, and who knows what else.

Tom didn't know much about coaching football, but he knew how to get guys psyched up to hit and knock people out on the football field.

This wasn't of any interest to Preston or me. We were finesse players. He tried it all the time with Leon, but Leon never had that killer instinct. John, on the other hand was Tom's kind of player, and they hit it off right away. John was a wild guy. Tom liked that.

John was from a middle class family that lived in the hills. He had lots of cash in his pockets, drove a fancy car and was always on the phone wheeling and dealing. Pretty girls flocked to John, and there always seemed to be a lot of other slick, well-dressed guys in nice cars coming in and out of the house. This was all fine with Tom.

I guess it isn't hard to figure out what John was up to in those days, but I was still a naive country boy, and I didn't want to know. In all the years I've known John, he never involved me in any of those dealings, and for the most part, he never tried to influence me in anything but positive ways.

Preston? For those first few months at Valley Prep, Preston was having the time of his life. He spent about the same amount of time in the classroom I did. Zero!

Preston was young and quiet, but he liked to party as much as my other roommates. He and Tom were having all kinds of fun together, and on the baseball diamond he was dominating. He spent most of his spare time with John, who showed him plenty of good times.

So when Jay called to ask how we were doing, Tom always told him, "Cool. Everything's cool."

In Tom's mind, everything was cool. He was savoring the lifestyle. Tom knew that if Jay had caught a glimpse of our living situation he would have thrown Valley Prep on its ear. His main job was to keep his brother away from the coaches. Tom knew that any trouble between Jay and the coaches would mean an end to his gravy train, so he handled conversations with his brother on a need-to-know basis.

20. SPRING

The media called the spring semester of my sophomore year at Valley Prep, the "Season of Hype."

Every day, the hype surrounding our team grew. The powerhouse team we were going to be; the championships we were going to win.

When spring training camp opened, the coaching staff discussed nothing else but college recruiters. They motivated us by dropping names of recruiters from big-time universities like Notre Dame and USC. On any given day, a dozen strangers lined the practice field to see what the hype was all about. We had better be at the top of our game when they arrived.

Sure enough, the colleges showed up on campus throughout the spring semester. The word quickly spread that Valley Prep was going to have one of the most explosive backfields in the history of the state. The media fed on it.

The greatest backfield of any small school in state history? That question just might be pondered after all of the results are in this fall as Valley Prep will show-case RB's Marcus Wright-Fair (6-2, 210) and Derek Sparks (6-0, 210), who rampaged for 2,900 yards between them last season. Sparks, remember, is a transfer who did his running at large school power Central of Long Beach and was the State Sophomore Player of the Year.

Wright-Fair ran last year for the Sundevils and is considered by some scouts as one of the state's top five RB prospects this year. As if that isn't enough, Valley

> *Prep head coach J.K. Santini will also have two other solid returnees in QB-LB Tarrance Metcalf (5-11, 190) and OT Don Donaldson (6-5, 260).*

Santini and Hutchinson treated us more like movie stars than athletes. We ate it up. I couldn't wait for the season to begin. I was ready to show all of these guys what I could do. I was so excited that it was hard for me to sleep at night.

One day Coach Santini drove some of his "blue chip" players like Marcus, John, Leon, Preston, and me to USC to meet the coaching staff and watch their spring workout.

I couldn't believe it. I was walking around the campus of the university I had been dreaming about my whole life. I was as giddy as a little kid when I walked by the bigger-than-life bronzed statue of Tommy Trojan on his horse, Traveler.

I couldn't do anything but smile when Coach took us out to the practice field and introduced us around. "C'mon fellas, I want you to meet a couple of people," he said.

He walked us up to the Trojan recruiting coordinator, Coach Bernardi, and Larry Smith, the head coach. We stood on the grass for a minute gawking before we could actually muster up any words.

Except for John, who immediately stepped forward. "I'm John Pearlman, butt kickin' hard hittin' linebacker." The men from USC enjoyed his spontaneity and chuckled as they shook his hand.

I managed to step forward. "My name's Derek Sparks."

Coach Smith laughed out loud and slapped his recruiter on the back. "Is this kid putting me on?" Then he spoke to me. "Oh, we know who you are, son. That was some season you had at Central last year. That wasn't a fluke was it?" He grinned and leaned in as if sharing a secret.

I couldn't believe it. The head coach of the USC Trojans knew my name and was following my career. I felt like I had just meet the president, and he already knew about me. Taken aback, I was almost speechless. "I .... uh...I don't think so," I said genuinely humbled by the compliment.

"Hell no, it was no fluke!" said John robustly. John had no fear. "And wait until you see what he's gonna do this year."

"Yeah, we're all going to rip it up." It was Marcus Wright-Fair. He was talking up the team, but we all sensed his disappointment.

The coaches had made a fuss over me without even saying a word to him yet. After all, he was a senior, the one who really needed the recruiters' attention.

Marcus and I held the same dream of running for USC and earning the coveted Heisman Trophy. Our main conversation had been about what it would be like to put on that crimson and gold uniform. To run the football where Anthony Davis, Marcus Allen, O.J. Simpson, Mike Garrett, and a countless list of other incredible running backs had run. From what I had seen, Marcus had what it took to join their ranks.

Fortunately for Marcus, the men from USC knew who he was. Once he stepped forward, they went out of their way to make him feel like he was a valued recruit.

I had no idea that all of this was illegal. This kind of conversation wasn't supposed to occur. But from my perspective it was a dream come true. I was grateful to my coach for making it happen.

Smith and Bernardi were also curious about Leon. They hadn't read about him the way they had about Marcus and me. They wanted to know what position he played, what kind of speed he had. It was an amazing visit.

As we were about to leave, Bernardi turned to John. "So, you're a linebacker? What are you weighing in at? About 190?"

"One ninety five," said John, who had already shot up from 185 to 195 in no time at all.

"Well, you look like a talented guy, but we like our linebackers to be more like 220 at least." As the two college coaches turned to walk away I could see the fire in John's eyes.

Bernardi paused and turned back to us. "Maybe we'll drop by your school in two or three weeks. Take a look at a workout."

"Until then," he said directly to me, "here's my card. Give me a call if I can be of any assistance. Keep yourselves out of trouble now."

They left us more excited than we had ever been in our lives.

The coaches were using this hype to get us focused and it was working. I became more focused on football than I had ever been. All I could think about was ways to have a better season, to gain more yards, to win more games. I worked out harder than ever before and every dream I had was about playing in the college and then the professional ranks.

The coaches wanted us totally committed to Valley Prep football. They assured us if we followed their lead, committed ourselves body and soul to their cause, we would cash in. We were hooked. Or, at least, I was. I ate, drank and slept Valley Prep football, spending less time than ever in the classroom.

Leon was motivated to play football, but I don't think he ever really understood the importance of the whole situation. He was always a step behind. People called him lazy, the coaches rode him, but I don't think Leon was a sloth. I think he was just strange. I didn't understand the things he did; they just didn't make sense.

I'm telling you, as great a player as he was, there was something different about that boy. His reaction to all the hype was, at best, slow.

Preston was too busy playing baseball, hanging out, and enjoying his new freedom to give the recruiters and school work much thought.

While I was digesting Coach Bernardi's every word, thinking about my scholarship to USC, Preston figured it would all happen in due time without much effort. His social life was the main thing he had on his mind.

A great deal of his enthusiasm vanished when the coaches threw him his first curve ball. He would be the team's starting quarterback.

Most people would have been thrilled, but Preston knew exactly what this meant for him. He was a tremendous athlete but he was no quarterback. He was a receiver. A great one.

Now the coaches wanted to make him the quarterback on a team with no intention of ever throwing the ball. After a long conversation with Uncle Jay he accepted the quarterback position, but he was never happy about it.

Who recruits a quarterback who can't complete a pass? Preston asked me why the school had really sent for him if they didn't need a receiver. I couldn't give him a good answer. It puzzled me too, but I was hooked on the hype.

"Just trust the coaches," I told him, dismissing the question. "They have to know what they're doing." I often wish I had never said that.

Marcus reaction to the entire situation was a different story. I have to hand it to Marcus. He carried himself with class, like a true team player, even though he was disgusted with what was going down.

Marcus had more to lose than any of us. He was one of the most talented seniors in the country, with this season being his last chance to post the kind of numbers he needed to attract a major university. Everybody knew he was a talent, but he couldn't afford for some other senior running back to finish with better statistics than him. He needed carries, a lot of them, and my arrival had done nothing to help his confidence.

His parents grew irate. They stormed down to the school and raised hell with the coaches. They threatened to pull Marcus out, and since I wasn't there, I'm sure the coaches reassured them that Marcus was their main man. I wasn't going to be any threat to him.

Anybody who read the newspapers would have to wonder if that was really going to be the case.

RUNNING SHARED
MARCUS WRIGHT-FAIR AND DEREK SPARKS TURN POTENTIAL RIVALRY INTO POWERFUL ALLIANCE AS TANDEM IN VALLEY PREP BACKFIELD

This fall at Valley Prep, an academically demanding college preparatory school in the San Gabriel Valley, great expectations will not be found only on required reading lists. They will be found on the football field where two standout running backs with an abundance of talent, senior Marcus Wright-Fair and junior fullback Derek Sparks, stand poised for high school greatness.

But it's not as if there's an inordinate amount of pressure associated with those expectations. Most of them are self imposed.

"Derek wants 1,000 yards in four games," Wright-Fair said with a smile, "and I want 1,000 in five games."

Let it further be noted that Sparks said that he would like to rush for 2,500 yards this season.

File this under the something-has-to-give department. The last time somebody checked, only one football was allowed on the field at a time. But that doesn't seem to faze these two backs, especially Sparks. He recalls the day this summer that he, along with Wright-Fair sat down with a piece of paper and worked out their season goals. His list topped that of Wright-Fair, the Valley's leading returning rusher. Sparks' great expectations drew a classic Hollywood double-take from Wright-Fair.

"Marcus looked at me," Sparks said, "and we looked at each other for a few seconds. He couldn't believe it. But it can be done."

Which, if you are a Valley Prep opponent this year is the most alarming possibility of all. It just might be done.

Are rival coaches aware?

"Unfortunately, I am," Village Coach David Logan said. "I think the whole world is."

In summation, we are supposed to look at these two players, both of whom rushed for more than 1,500 yards last season, and try to believe that there's going to be no trouble when it comes to egos, play calling and piling up the stats?

The answer from the head of the Valley Prep program is a resounding yes.

"There was every chance in the world for a negative rivalry to develop," said Coach Santini, the immediate beneficiary of this wealth of talent. "But those two have become very good friends and very supportive of one another."

Welcome to Sundevil football. The situation is such that two Division I bound running backs can become good friends and not only learn how to share the ball, but plan to enjoy it thoroughly.

"When one runs, the other blocks, happily," Santini said, beaming.

This budding powerhouse backfield began to take shape at the end of the last school year when Sparks visited Valley Prep with his uncle, Jay Sparks, and expressed interest in transferring.

Coach J.K. Santini had dealt with transfers before. But as he was soon to learn, Derek Sparks was no ordinary transfer.

Sparks was leaving the program at Central, one of the state's best in football, after a stunning season. The 6-0, 210-pound fullback rushed for 1,494 yards and 15 touchdowns.

He was an All-City selection.

He was named State Sophomore Player of the Year by Cal-Hi Sports.

Sparks wanted to play football at Valley Prep, a Division IX school.

"At first I said, oh, that'll be great. A fullback. That's good for me," Wright-Fair recalled with a laugh.

Then, however, Wright-Fair found out just who Sparks was.

"I was shocked," Wright-Fair said, still smiling.

I know Marcus was angry. But he didn't let it show and he never took it out on me. We both made it a point to say the right things to the press, but neither one of us felt this was an ideal situation. Under the circumstances, we thought the best thing to do was what the coaches wanted. Just run the football.

◆◆◆

John had gone crazy since meeting the coaches at USC. His life consisted of working out, eating and partying. Those were the only activities his mind could process.

When the USC coaches visited our school two-and-a-half weeks later, John had ballooned up to over 200 pounds. His bench press had increased substantially and he was huge. His face was a big, wild looking acne-riddled thing.

I guess I knew what John was doing to buff up, but I didn't think about it. No one ever talked to me about steroids and they'd never approached me about using them. I had plenty of size already for a running back. And I'm sure that no one wanted to deal with Jay's reaction if he'd caught wind of something like that.

I don't approve of what John and several of my teammates decided to do behind closed doors. Steroids are real, illegal, and lethal. But here again, it was a situation where a high school teenager wanted it all. He had the coach's assurance that he had what it took to go all the way to the big leagues. With their help he could play for the greatest college in the country and advance into the professional ranks.

But this student-athlete is missing one critical ingredient. These schools need guys who are bigger than you. Guys who bench press 400 pounds.

"You want those recruiters to approach you?" Coach Hutchinson asked John. "If you do, you gotta do whatever it takes. There's a price you have to pay to be the best. Just remember, this is a once in a lifetime chance."

The kid knew that he was heading into rough territory, but he wanted that dream! When his coaches tossed clichés and dangled promises, he figured that they were offering him the magic potion for success.

I don't agree with it, but I see how it happens. And it's happening everywhere. All over the country, kids who aren't doing steroids are looking at guys who do and wondering how they're going to compete against them.

John was a maniac, hell bent on winning and impressing the college recruiters. When those guys walked onto our campus, and reassessed John, their jaws almost hit the ground. He had become bigger, crazier, faster and more agile. They liked what they saw and they let John know it. They did everything but question his methods.

They liked what they saw in me too. I was in seventh heaven. One recruiter pulled me aside and said, "You have scholarship written all over you. I could get you a scholarship right now if you are ready to commit."

I didn't know if he was just blowing smoke, but signing a letter of intent early was an option I couldn't allow myself to consider.

I could see myself explaining that to Uncle Jay. "I'm thinking about skipping the recruiting process and committing to play for USC."

Jay wouldn't have said a word. He would have just thrown me into a straight-jacket.

Besides, I saw those same coaches pulling Marcus Wright-Fair aside, giving him the same song and dance. They played with our young minds and I believe they enjoyed every minute of it.

It was all hype, set on a platter, all-you-can-eat. We devoured our helpings and waited for the next serving. This was Valley Prep, and here hype was sold by the pound.

RICARDO DeARATANHA / Los Angeles Times

Derek Sparks of Valley Prep rushed for 1,394 yards and 15 touchdowns at Central last fall.

21. SUMMER

We were all anxious to begin the football season. The strength of our team and the resources available at Valley Prep made me view my dreams as foregone conclusions.

We needed to turn this season into an unbelievable one. We needed to gain more yards, score more touchdowns and win more games than ever in the school's history. And we would! We were sure of it!

I don't remember ever getting a report card, but they told me that I had a 3.0 grade point average. In my book that was good enough. The machine was taking care of things. I kept my eyes shut and my ears plugged. I just ran the football.

What should have opened my eyes the widest was not my own grades, but the grades of those around me. Preston, who was receiving passing marks, didn't even know where his classrooms were. And John. He had passing grades in everything. Chemistry, Algebra, Spanish. Spanish! Let me tell you, if John could have counted *uno, dos, tres,* it would have impressed me.

John was a sharp guy, but that boy didn't know any more Spanish than I knew Portuguese, yet he passed with flying colors.

John had a lot of help. He had won the favor of the football coaching staff. To them he was the consummate linebacker; a wild, aggressive kid who had no fear. He was willing to do as told—legal or not—to help bring a championship to our school. He had proved that he knew how high the stakes were and what lines he had to cross.

John thought he was acting like a team player. Just a regular stand up guy. Maybe even macho. The truth is he was acting stupid. John took those injections with the same ease that he swallowed the coaches' bull. He didn't give a second thought to the consequences of either.

John was a renegade who played the game with a ferocious, reckless intensity. As a coach, Tom loved John's style of play and made sure John got his due. John was Tom's *boy*. If someone messed with John, they messed with Tom too, and no one wanted to mess with Tom.

This was going to be the season of our dreams. No one doubted it, except for Jay. His relationship with the coaches had grown tense by the end of the spring semester. By summer, the friction was insufferable.

Jay was not a man afraid to express his opinions and he felt that he was being wronged. He had some serious issues with the coaches.

Jay had trusted Tom to keep him informed about Preston and me. Tom and the coaches reassured him constantly that everything was going according to the plan. Our best interests were their first priority.

Their statements were plastic, though, and all they really accomplished was to amplify Jay's anger. He began to make surprise occasional visits to the campus. It mortified him to discover Preston and me out of class, hanging out, talking to college recruiters. We were enjoying every campus activity aside from studying.

Jay raced into the coaches' office and demanded answers. The coaches nodded to Jay, called us in and admonished us sternly. "What have we told you guys about this? You better get to class!"

When they felt that their explanations had appeased Jay, they forgot about the matter. A week later Jay returned to campus, found us out of class and again resumed breathing fire at the coaching staff.

The coaches weren't used to someone like Jay—a black guy who wasn't even a coach—walking in on them and carrying on like he owned the place. They had a football program to run, and Jay's tirades made no sense to them. They were ensuring our futures and, after all, things were being taken care of.

Jay screamed at them, "You're not taking care of these boys' education! They need to learn. They need to be in class. What happens when you all are through with them, huh? Are you gonna take care of them when you've got a whole new crop of young kids in here and these boys can't even fill out a job application?"

"Jay, you may not see it, but we're looking at the big picture. The long haul." To them, Jay was too simple a man to realize their master plan.

Valley Prep was a stepping stone, at least for Coach Hutchinson. He knew that if he could deliver his players to a major university he could negotiate a coaching job for himself as well. He saw his new position as a finder's fee and he didn't need some player's uncle getting in his face, telling him how to run his program.

Jay could have cared less about the coaching staff's career ambitions. "To hell with that," Jay spat back. "I'm here for what's best for these boys. Not just today, but in the future. And I've seen how you guys operate.

"Let some new kid come along from Arkansas or Nebraska who looks like a better meal ticket, you'll sell my nephews down the river without a second thought.

"Now, you came to me and made me an offer, and I've done my part. I brought these boys here and let you fix the deck on your football team, get the media falling all over you, and that's fine. But if you think you're going to push me out of the picture, grab control of these boys' minds and ruin their futures, you better think again." Jay was livid.

"I brought these boys two thousand miles for an opportunity, and I'm not gonna let them be denied. They won't be treated like the Wright-Fairs."

"Ruin their futures?" Coach Hutchinson, usually affable, turned red with rage. He wasn't going to sit still and let Jay attack his gameplan.

"Listen pal, we took those kids out of the piece-of-crap neighborhood they came from and gave them the best money can buy.

"You want them to stay stuck in the projects?" he said staring Jay down. "You're the one who's trying to hold them back. Do you know how many major college recruiters we've introduced these kids to already? If you want them to land scholarships to the best colleges in the country, back off and let us do our jobs!"

Then he sank back in his chair, cupping his hands behind his head, and smiled. "Now, if you want them to scrub carpets for a living, keep interfering!"

That was a low blow. Jay didn't need a reminder that he hadn't lived up to his potential. He was more aware of it than Hutchinson could ever realize. Jay's haunting was of the talent he'd been blessed with and lost. No one knew better than him, the hard life he was leading.

It made Jay question whether he was doing the right thing. He had allowed the coaches to bend the rules. He also knew that he couldn't afford to support Preston, his brother Tom, and me.

We had been living on the private school campus for months now without even the trace of a bill. Tuition, books, housing, all of those expenses were taken care of. The little things I had hit Jay up for before, at Central, were not a problem at Valley Prep.

With Preston now in the equation, Jay was at Valley Prep's financial mercy. He had promised our mothers that he would see to our education. Now he had to ask himself if he could really show us the American dream from his carpet cleaning van?

Still, he was trying to retain some dignity.

By this time, though, we were all fresh out of dignity. The coaches lost their dignity by recruiting players out of their own self-interest in violation of every rule in the books. There wasn't much dignity in running a sports program that existed only in the pursuit of championships and notoriety.

And, for the players of the game, there wasn't any dignity in pocketing cash we hadn't earned or living in a house we weren't paying for.

In the end, nobody retained any dignity or self-respect.

The coaches swore up and down that they knew what they were doing. They would make sure that we went to class.

Jay wasn't satisfied, but he could only raise so much hell. He had other axes to grind.

Jay was concerned about who I was hanging out with. He'd come by the campus and seen me ride up with John in his Mustang convertible 5.0, shiny chrome wheels and tinted windows. Jay was familiar with those show cars and he knew the lifestyle that went with them. Plus, taking one look at John, Jay was convinced that something foul was going on.

One day Jay caught me driving Coach Santini's Porsche. I was barely 16 and didn't have a driver's license. He worried that I was turning into a degenerate at Valley Prep. I wasn't as bad as Jay imagined, but it was easy to understand why he got upset.

He threatened to pull me out of school if nobody took action. For starters, he wanted the coaches to keep me away from John Pearlman.

Hardly anyone could understand how John and I had become such close friends. It was true that he was into all kinds of dealings that I didn't have a clue about. I was from the country and John was a city boy. Although our personalities were as different as day and night, in several ways we were alike.

As I got to know him, it became clear that we were both driven by the same desperate need to be somebody.

John's real father disappeared when he was young, and like me, he was trying to prove that he was someone who was worth staying for.

He was living with us on campus because his mother and stepdad felt that he was out of control and they were tired of butting heads. He was increasingly moody and hard to deal with.

John was wild, but he had a great sense of humor. I was a serious kid and John kept me laughing. He taught me how to relax and to enjoy life. I needed people like John around me.

He also swears to this day that he taught me how to dress. John always made fun of the home-stitched sweaters I brought from Texas. But heck, I didn't know anything about fashion. What I wore seemed fine to me.

Beneath that glossy surface smile, John was all heart. I think he really wanted to be around me as well, in hopes that some of my values might rub off on him.

I've got to say that John was always respectful and he never pushed any of his shady dealings on me. Besides laughing a lot, we talked football. We were both on a mission to make the game our lives.

Jay didn't see John the way I did. All he could see was the car, the money, the thick face and neck, and the show John put on everywhere he went..

◆◆◆

John Pearlman and I shared one passion that drew us into a close friendship — football.

Nothing set Jay off like the SAT, the entrance exam required of everyone applying to college. It's a tough exam, even for kids who go to class every day.

Jay wanted me to get it out of the way early, so that the college recruiters would be assured of my eligibility and they'd have no questions about my grades.

John, who did everything the coaches told him, was the first to get his out of the way. The minimum passing grade was 700, and the national average was somewhere just under 1,000, out of a possible 1,600 points, which you'd have to be some kind of genius to get even close to. John scored 1,200.

How did he do it? A guy who openly admitted to reading on a sixth grade level? Simple. He didn't take the SAT.

The school worked it out for an honors student to carry John's ID and take the test. The kid probably pocketed a wad of cash, John got his score, and the school got away with another violation. John, however, lost another piece of himself.

John didn't care, he went around strutting and laughing, calling himself Einstein, and flashing his 1,200 score.

It only took Jay a second to figure out what had happened. He didn't like it.

Rather than confront the coaches again he came straight to me. "Derek, you better start cramming because I just picked up an application for you to take the SAT and I'll be personally escorting you to the test center."

It wasn't the best news he could have brought me, but he was right. I was a decent student. I may have had my work cut out for me, but I told myself that all I had to do was apply myself.

I got to work studying as best I could. Besides having my hands full, I had trouble concentrating on anything besides football. But still I worked hard and did the best I could.

Jay pulled Tom aside and explained in detail how important this test was. He made Tom promise to keep anyone from distracting me from my studies. So Tom stood over me and kept his promise.

I was so fatigued and overloaded on the day of the exam, it felt as though my head was stuffed with cotton.

Jay drove me to the junior college where it was being administered. He looked at me hard before I walked in. All he said, was, "Do the best you can."

I guess the wait for the results was probably a tense time for Jay. I didn't give it a thought. When my scores came in, I opened the envelope like it was just another piece of mail. I didn't make any ceremony out of it; I just ripped the envelope open.

Below the minimum score, I had failed. It hurt; I was a failure. I fumbled, big time!

Jay wasn't laughing either. He went straight to the coaches' office and threw the scores down on the desk, shouting in their faces. Coach Santini and Hutchinson didn't appreciate his approach at all. It didn't take long for the whole thing to turn into an ugly shouting match.

The three of them went at it for a long time. It ended with the coaches telling Jay that he was overreacting. I still had two years to retake the test. They said they could get me the best tutors around and I would pass the next time with ease. Jay didn't believe them for a second, but he left it at that. He had another agenda. Jay went to see Tom.

Jay placed a big chunk of the blame upon Tom's shoulders. He said that Tom should have seen what was going on and reported it to him. He felt that the coaches were manipulating Tom. He couldn't stomach the thought of Tom siding with strangers, against him.

Tom, who had always been a most loyal family member, took Jay's insult badly. His creed had always been: Blood is thicker than water, and he felt that he had done a good job watching over us.

Tom was also in agreement with the coaches: I had two years to retake the SAT; Jay was overreacting; and things weren't as bad as they appeared.

Most of all, Tom didn't like anybody, not even his brother, getting in his face and yelling at him. Especially in front of us kids. On the street he would have put somebody in the hospital for that.

That day the two brothers, Jay and Tom, got into it real bad, to the point where we had to jump in and pull them apart. Their relationship was never the same again.

Jay left the house in a huff, but he wasn't through. He was, in fact, just getting started. Jay was going to the top.

22. THE TEXAS CONNECTION

Jay went to Pop Wilson, the founder and principal of the school, and laid out his complaints about the coaches at Valley Prep. He knew Wilson was aware of the situation. The two had spoken before, not only about the deal for Preston and me, but about his role in the future of the school.

The "Texas Connection" was Jay's lifetime dream. He was looking for a deal that allowed him to bring talented athletes from Texas to Valley Prep, where the kids could receive a better education, solid training, and be seen by recruiters from the major universities.

Wilson figured that if the talent level of these kids was anywhere near Preston's or mine, this program would be a gold mine in no time. He granted Jay his full support and urged him to begin work immediately.

Jay's vision was even bigger. He saw a large residence, with all the amenities, that could house these boys. It would be funded, of course, by the school and friends of the program.

Jay would supervise the development of these young athletes, steer them towards a major university and become known as the man to see in the world of high school athletics.

Jay saw the Texas Connection as a great way to help a lot of good kids. He also saw it as a way to finally make a name for himself.

Jay was the baseball player who didn't make it. This was his chance to leave that sense of failure behind. The Texas Connection would be his legacy.

If, however, Jay was unable to have singular control over these kids, he would refuse to bring any of them to the West Coast. He knew that the coaches thought of him as a control freak. He was willing to accept that, so long as his dream didn't get compromised.

Pop Wilson was smart. He didn't deal directly with the issues at hand. Instead, he talked about Jay's Texas Connection and how important an idea it was. He discussed potential investors for Jay's housing facility. Basically, he poured on the hype. He laid it on so thick that Jay had stars in his eyes.

Then Coach Santini stepped in, assuring Jay that the plan was under consideration. "Pop Wilson will be spending the summer streamlining and making preparations for your new position within the school," he said. He pleaded with Jay to allow the semester to end peacefully.

Jay left the meeting feeling that he'd done all he could; but he couldn't shake a terrible feeling in his gut. He had no alternative but to wait and see if Pop Wilson would make good on his promises. If he didn't wait, Jay would never know if he had overreacted with the coaches. He would never know for sure which side of the fence they were really sitting on.

I don't know if Jay saw it, but at that moment, he had made one more concession to the machine. And like it or not, this made him a little more a part of it.

Tom's reaction, to prove to his brother that he did have us under control, was to become tougher on us. While he never encouraged us to crack the books, he was a real driver about football.

There wasn't much Tom could say to me; all I did was think about football. Preston, though, was still coming down from his baseball season, and wasn't at all happy about becoming a quarterback. Preston got the worst of it.

Tom stayed on Preston day and night. And when Tom got on you, it could be unbearable. He shouted, got in your face, pushed and grabbed you, and hurled insults at you until you broke.

He wanted a response and the only way he knew to provoke it was by challenging you.

Tom's methods made Preston uneasy. He didn't understand his uncle's cruel words or how he could turn on him as he had. "This is sports, not slavery," Preston shouted at Tom. "It's just a game!" To him, he should have been enjoying his high school experience, not enduring it.

Preston began to stay away from the house as much as he could. He was hanging out with a guy on the team named Steve Cebrian. Steve was bad news and I knew that it wouldn't be long before my cousin was introduced to something he really wasn't ready for.

Preston, who just started drinking when he came to Valley Prep, was now putting it away with the best of them. I prayed that he would use good judgment, but I couldn't do much to stop him.

Preston and I still got along great, but things had changed. He hated getting hassled by Tom, while I received preferential treatment because I was Derek Sparks, State Player of the Year.

Fortunately, Preston and I both found relief from the stress when we received an invitation to the Terry Donahue Football Camp at UCLA, paid for by Valley Prep. For a while we were as happy as we had been when Preston first arrived.

It was thrilling to meet alumni players, like quarterback Troy Aikman, defensive back James Washington and linebacker Ken Norton, all Dallas Cowboys who came out to support the program.

I was blown away by the number of people—coaches and players—who knew who I was and had memorized my stats.

Preston, though, was wallowing in perpetual anonymity. His name was obscured within the coaching circles, and only a few other players at the camp knew who he was. It hurt him, and it bothered me too.

I kept thinking, "If they only knew how good he really is."

Preston was a far better all-around athlete than I was and he deserved the recognition. But ever since he had arrived in California, everywhere we went we heard "Derek Sparks...oh yeah, and his cousin Preston." After a while this would get to anybody, regardless of their talent or confidence.

Our talent and confidence were boosted by coaches from other Southern California high schools who cornered us, offering us a better life and all the perks that we'd been getting at Valley Prep. All they required was that we transfer.

Football was an innocent game to us. For these coaches it was strictly business.

Still, we had a lot of fun at the camp. We learned a ton about the game and met people who would certainly impact our futures.

I was walking on air when Terry Donahue, the head coach, and some of the UCLA staff complemented my abilities as a talented running back. I felt all of my dreams coming together and only an arm's length away.

It was an amazing week of non-stop action; but the best moment arrived at the end. I was chosen runner-up to the camp MVP. It was a great honor—to be given this distinction amongst the finest high school football players in the country—and I knew it could only help my recruiting value.

Then they announced the camp MVP. Preston Sparks!

I was so happy for him I didn't know what to do. I just hugged him and grinned. He tried to play it off like it was no big deal, but I knew better. I knew he was proud of himself. It was probably the only time in his life he had come in ahead of me. It was just what he needed to build his self-esteem.

23. PADS

Spring football. Full pads, full contact. We became so pumped for it you'd have thought it was the season opener. This was the time for the players to claim their positions. There were no guarantees. It didn't matter if a guy had been around for a year or two; this year was new and everything was up for grabs.

Marcus Wright-Fair knew this better than anyone. Here was a guy who had proved himself time and time again. He had brought a lot of glory to the team and to the school. But because I was there, he knew he would have to prove himself all over again.

Marcus knew he had a position on the team. So did I. But how many times in a game would each of us get to carry the football? This is where we'd have to settle the matter, out here on the practice field, months before the first game.

The returning offensive linemen were riled. They knew that Leon's arrival put everyone's position in jeopardy. If he was all they thought he was, he'd take someone's spot, and the coaches would move people around to accommodate him.

There was another new guy, Don Donaldson—6-foot-5, 260-pounds, and mean—who had transferred from Washington High. His unexpected arrival put another position up for grabs.

Then, there was Marcus Wright-Fair's little brother, Cedrick, determined to make himself feel more valuable than his brother had been. Everyone was ready to go.

Nobody, but nobody, felt more pumped than John Pearlman. He was in a zone all of his own. He had blown up to 225-pounds, bigger and wilder than ever.

Tom provoked him, taking him even higher, knowing exactly which buttons to push. "You ain't nothing, Pearlman. You're a woosh!" he screamed. "Ray Jackson is gonna eat you for breakfast. He's gonna hit you one time and send you cryin' back home to yo mama in the hills."

Ray Jackson was a returning linebacker who had had a big season the previous year. John was basically a walk-on without a position. The fact he had played only "B" ball at Grant Hills made him even less of a threat. Everyone considered Ray a sure thing. They looked at him as *the man* on defense.

I hadn't spoken with John the few days before the first practice. He was *that* focused. We found out later that John had popped about fifteen painkillers before he left the locker room. By the time we hit the field John was amped.

When it came time for the first hitting drill, John wanted to get the confrontation on in a hurry. He squared off against Ray Jackson, making them the first hitters in the drill.

When the whistle blew, John let out a yelp that sounded like some kind of jungle battle cry. As he catapulted towards Ray, his war-cry rose to a crescendo. At the point of impact, the collision sounded more like a train wreck than a football hit. Ray's helmet flew clear off his head, knocking him immediately unconscious. He laid on the ground in a gigantic heap with John screaming and growling over him.

Jackson was done for the day, and Valley Prep had a new middle linebacker. For the rest of the day nobody wanted to go against John. Some players fell to the ground just to avoid being bulldozed by him. By the end of the day John was the center of the Valley Prep defense.

That night, the pills wore off. I was in a fright watching John; hyper, sweaty and restless. No position is worth your health. John was incapable of coping with the drugs and steroids and their terrible side-effects. Nobody is.

Preston's debut as quarterback was less impressive. He was a nervous wreck. From his first miscue, Tom was all over him. Preston struggled to keep his cool and remain focused. It was a bad outing, but there was no question that Preston was going to be our starting quarterback.

The returning quarterback, Tarrance Metcalf, had had an even better baseball season than Preston, so he decided to concentrate on his baseball efforts.

The team had won the state championship, and Tarrance had baseball recruiters clamoring to get his attention. Even with all the pressure the football coaches put on him to play, he wanted no part of it. Preston was *the man*.

But it was the match-up in the backfield everybody was waiting to see. It was the kind of moment I had spent my whole life preparing for. Marcus Wright-Fair was ready too.

It was an unbelievable day and we were untouchable. Marcus put on a show with a fancy move. I answered back with one just as pretty. He took a big hit and broke a tackle; I busted one up the middle. If I showed strength with a crushing block, Marcus came right back and laid somebody out. That day we were both everything a running back should have been, and more.

The biggest challenge I had was during a sweep play against the defense. The moment I thought I had broken it, they leveled me from my blind side. It rattled my teeth, and, for a second, I thought I'd blacked out. I stayed conscious, though, only to look up and see John Pearlman growling like a beast. We were friends, but this was warfare, and John meant business.

It was war. It was set up like a game, but we all knew that we were fighting for our futures and our lives. Ten years from now, if our families were not living in nice homes with fancy cars in the driveways, we would always look back to this day and the ones that followed, wondering on which day we had dropped the ball.

We were kids, but we had put on men's clothes and stepped onto a battlefield baring men's equipment. Even amongst ourselves there was no negotiation. Show off or be shown up. Eat or be eaten. Our coaches loved every minute of it.

When it came time for timed sprints, 40-yard dashes, all of the attention turned to Marcus and me again. The papers had been saying all along we both had 4.5 speed, and now the whole team wanted to see who actually had the jets.

We ran stride for stride, Marcus 4.6, me 4.6, Marcus 4.5, me 4.5. When we both crossed the line at 4.4, the whole team exploded. We both had to give each other out of breath high-fives.

Practices went on like that for three weeks. The intensity never let up. Although he was a little slow to catch on, Leon Lett proved he was the kind of player the coaches had hoped he'd be. The new guy, Donaldson, cemented a spot for himself. Cedrick Wright-Fair hammered his way into the defensive starting line as well. Even though this was only spring workouts, we were looking like a formidable team.

24. Two-A-Days

If the season opener is heaven, the weeks before it are definitely hell. Some teams actually call it "Hell Week." We called it "Two-a-Days." Two practices each day — from the first light of day to crawling into bed at night.

Wake up call was 7 a.m. Morning practice ran from eight until eleven. Three hours of conditioning, agility drills, hitting and play execution, all with ruthless intensity. It felt like the whole practice was running, running and more running.

Two-a-Days occurred in August, the dead of summer, the hottest days of the year. They delivered the last chance a player had to earn a starting position or simply to make the team.

Most players didn't give a thought to preparing for the season. If they were smart they spent the whole summer getting in shape for Two-a-Days.

During that time, before Two-a-Days, no one partied. We didn't go out and we didn't talk to anyone. We just chilled, saving whatever energy we had.

We told our friends and family to forget about us for a while. We told them to pretend that we didn't exist. With what we were going through, we didn't have the time, strength, or desire to deal with anyone. It took too much energy just wondering if we were going to live through the next practice.

Two-a-Days started with testing. The coaches wanted to see what kind of shape we were in. They began with timed 60-yard shuttle runs. Not just once or twice, but again and again and again, with next to no rest in between.

For those players who didn't register quick times, the coaches stuck their names on the *out-of-shape* list. That was guaranteed to get them in shape.

Those out of shape players were pulled out of bed every morning at six o'clock, one hour before the rest of the squad. They were drug onto the field and made to run the shuttle until they passed it.

By the time the rest of the team hit the field, those guys were already dead tired. For the remainder of the practice they were tackling dummies for the other athletes trying to make a name for themselves.

Hitting drills were the real eye opener for me. We were one-on-one. One guy has the ball, the other has the growl. There's no going around or outside of the cones. You take it straight down the line.

The team's best players were expected to jump into the drill first. If we didn't, the rest of the squad thought you had no heart. Boys who hesitated too long got nicknames like "wosh" and "puss" (And it's not really "puss" they were saying, either). Nobody wanted to go through the season carrying nicknames like that.

Next, are position drills. Linemen with linemen, running backs with running backs. You are judged on every move, and everything is filmed for the coaches to review later. The cameras, we call "Eye in the Sky," own you. If you let up for one second, the *eye* will be there to make note of it, and the next day a coach will be breathing down your neck. You ease up for a second, and there's another guy on the team who wants your spot, and is going to make you pay.

Run a play. Hit. Sprint. Hit. Agility drills. Hit. Learn new plays. Hit. Eight laps around the field. Hit, hit, hit. By now, the sun is beating down and you're hot and dead tired. Your dry mouth is cracked and feels like cotton. Your body is dehydrated. There's a small mud puddle in the corner of the field that begins to look good to you.

You think about faking an injury. Anything, just for a few minutes rest. But it would give the next guy the chance to shine, and you can't allow that to happen if you want a spot on the team. So you run some more, hit some more, on and on.

The whistle finally blows to end the first practice of the day. After a brief speech from the head coach, the players are dismissed for a two hour lunch break. At three o'clock we'll do it all over again until six. During that lunch break you don't know whether to eat or sleep. They are the two urges that will gnaw at you for the remaining two weeks.

By the afternoon practice it feels like an accomplishment just to get into your pads. When you hit the field, it's on again. One hundred percent intensity and focus are required. Nothing less is expected. Or accepted. No matter how hard you push yourself, it's never enough.

At Valley Prep, they did it for two weeks instead of one. During those weeks you learn where your limits are and what it takes to go beyond them. That's part of the beauty of being an athlete that most people don't understand. There's something about the power to push your body beyond its limits, to keep going when every nerve ending is screaming for you to give up. It confirms that there's more to the game than just brute strength or agility.

When the final Two-a-Day session is over, it's time to begin the season. The players look at each other differently. You've been to hell and back together and discovered a strength you never even knew was there. As you stand amongst your teammates, the ones that you trust to watch your back, the ones that fought through the pain, you almost wish the whole thing could continue. For just a few minutes you feel invincible.

25. ROLL

The Valley Prep Sundevils were ready to roll. Having constructed their dream team, all our coaches had to do now was to put us on the field and see how we would respond. We were ready.

Some people around the league felt we were too ready. There was a flood of negative press about the way Valley Prep did things, right up to the opening kickoff.

> **VALLEY PREP SHAPING UP AS BULLY ON BLOCK**
>
> *What do you get when you take senior tailback Marcus Wright-Fair, a Division I prospect who rushed for 1,514 yards last season; junior Derek Sparks, last season's State Sophomore Player of the Year at Central high; and junior quarterback Preston Sparks, a swift, talented transfer from Texas, and put them all in the same backfield?*
>
> *A) Countless rushing plays.*
>
> *B) Gobs of yardage on the ground.*
>
> *C) A slobbering coach.*
>
> *D) All of the above.*
>
> *OK, so that was easy "D" is the obvious choice. But there's more to this test.*

What do you get if you take the same trio and put them in the lethal blue uniform at Valley Prep and tell them to run wild on the apparently overmatched schools of the WAC League?

A) Angry rival coaches.

B) Defiant rival coaches.

C) Retreating rival coaches.

D) A league race that could be over before it starts.

E) All of the above.

Fill in the bubble by "E" and then take pity on the coaches at Eastern Christian, L.A. Christian, Southern, Western, and Village, who must face the mighty Sundevils this year. Valley Prep is ranked number one by the Southern Section in Division 9, and features what California Football magazine argues is perhaps "the best backfield in any small school in state history..."

...Some coaches may look at these numbers and turn white at the thought of tangling with the Sundevils. Others turn red with anger.

"As far as I'm concerned, Valley Prep is the best team money can buy," Eastern Christian Coach Mike Petrizzo said. "Year in and year out, 10 to 12 athletes show up that weren't there before. It drives me crazy that these new kids keep showing up, and they keep getting away with it."

I was more than a little worried when I started reading these things. It seemed to me that if everyone was already asking questions about how Valley Prep had acquired all of its great players, it would only be a matter of time before the correct answers appeared.

The coaches weren't worried though. At this, they were the masters. They covered their tracks well and always said exactly the right things to the press.

"If you're a good football coach," Coach Hutchinson says, "and have the bonus of being at a great school like Valley Prep, people find out where you are. Santini and I never leave the campus. We sit here and people say, 'Hey, what do we have to do to get into Valley Prep?' "

They had their lines down. They even had some of us believing it.

Coach Santini said, "If I had a kid who was a concert violinist, and I knew of a school in the Valley that sent more kids to Julliard than any other school, I'd send him there. The kids here get a great education and go on to play college athletics. That is the very reason why parents send their kids to Valley Prep."

A couple of smoothies. By this time I had myself actually believing that I came to Valley Prep to get a better education. I kept telling myself, repeating over and over, that down the line I would study harder and go to class more often. I told myself I was just under the pressure of adjusting to a new school and learning a new system.

Deep down in my heart I knew something was wrong. I just didn't have the time to spend thinking about it. That's not it; I didn't want to think about it. So I pushed it out of my mind and focused on the game, running the football and enjoying all the perks that came with it.

From the onset, we were too powerful for the WAC League teams. Our offense was overwhelming. Marcus and I ran circles around the opposing defenses. Preston contributed a slew of touchdowns. Our defense was crippling.

We shut out L.A. Jordan, the first team we played, 37-0. They never knew what hit them. Marcus and I played well together. I wasn't too disappointed with the number of carries I had. I don't know how Marcus felt about it, but he gained a ton of yards and scored a couple of touchdowns.

Our defense caught fire behind John Pearlman. Every time their offense attempted to move the ball we punished them for it.

The next couple of games followed in the same vein. We dismantled Bishop, 61-0.

After three games I had already scored ten touchdowns and Marcus had scored eight. We were both satisfied with the stats we were racking up. We even returned kickoffs, a coaches' ploy to give us more carries. It didn't work though; we were only seeing one kickoff a game. The other teams never scored.

Preston wasn't having the greatest time at quarterback. Tom was riding him hard. How exciting could it be, handing off to Marcus and me, watching us run away with it? Every now and then Preston got his chance on an option play. He scored from wherever he was.

I think it was somewhere around the week before our fourth game, when one reporter was talking to me about the season I was having, gushing compliments. Toward the end of the conversation, as I was leaving, I heard him laugh and say, "Imagine, if they put a runner like you at tailback! That would be like watching a highlight tape."

I smiled and walked away, but something was nagging at me. Later, in my room, as I thought about it, the truth hit me. I couldn't see why I had never thought about it before.

I was the Valley Prep fullback, a position that, in most systems, is predominately a blocking back. I had played fullback at Central, but not because I wanted to play that position, but because Keith Walker was the man, and I had been a last minute replacement. No one, at any other school, would have asked me to play as a fullback.

Marcus was the senior. The team was playing well and both of us were racking up big-time statistics. I knew this, but I still couldn't shake my thoughts.

What if a major university thought I was playing fullback because I couldn't cut it at tailback? I was being egotistical; I was thinking selfishly. But the truth was that a scholarship to a Division I school held all importance to me. A big part of me was having problems with Marcus being seen as the man.

Our fourth game of the season was against Bassett, a well-regarded team, but not ranked in the top ten, as we were. It was an important game for a lot of reasons. I was coming in with 490 yards, a great total, but nowhere near the 1,000 mark. I had to have a good game.

It's funny, Marcus seemed real up for the game too. Evidently I hadn't been the only one doing some thinking that week. Everything came down to the end zone. All the recruiters, all of the media, standing behind the chalk-line, waiting to snap a picture and hand us scholarship offers. Marcus and I stared at each for a minute, and then straight ahead.

Bassett had a running back named Marshawn Thomas who was on fire that year. His 584 rushing yards in three games put Marcus and me to shame. We both needed to have a big game to keep people from saying Thomas had "Put Out the Sparks" or "Marched Over Marcus," or whatever the media would come up with.

Both teams came out firing. The defenses, though, were putting their brand on the game. The Bassett defense played extremely well. Our defense responded, and as the first quarter ticked away, there was no score.

Then, late in the first, Marcus and I each broke off good size runs. Before we knew it, we had mounted a 43 yard drive to the 18-yard line. It was third down; Marcus and I both wanted the ball.

The coaches must have sensed that one of us would get upset if we didn't get the call because they sent in a pass play.

On most teams that wouldn't be unusual, but at Valley Prep, we never passed. Preston just uttered, "Huh?"

The play called for a "Play Action," where the tailback faked the hand-off and pretended to run the ball with me charging into the line to block the linebacker. Once the defense figured that neither of us had the ball, they'd scramble to recover. That's when the fullback would flare out and set-up to catch a pass. It was usually good for five or six yards. But it wouldn't be enough for a first down in this situation. We'd have to settle for a field goal attempt.

I crashed into the line and popped the outside linebacker pretty good. I always liked to hit. I didn't want him to think I was a potential receiver, so I held my block. Preston knew my moves; we were in synch all the way. It didn't matter if the deep receivers were covered or not. Preston had no faith in his ability to throw deep. I cut to the outside, and just as I turned to look back at Preston, the football was there. I tucked it away and made a quick cut to avoid the defensive back. After I accelerated, I saw the free safety closing in. I used my best move, twisting my upper body to freeze him. Then, with some contact, I made him feel that he had the tackle. Within a split second, I twisted away as hard as I could, spun a 360-turn, and changed directions at the same time. The momentum carried him to my right, just enough for me to break away with a straight-arm, pick up speed and it was off to the races.

Unfortunately for me, the move put me just off balance enough where I couldn't regain my original position. The free safety was able to save a touchdown, but not before I had gained 15 yards and the first down. First-and-goal from the 3-yard line.

Back in the huddle, the guys asked, "How did you do that?" I just shrugged and tried to get myself ready for the next play.

The call came in. It was "24 Power" with Marcus carrying, me blocking. Marcus literally walked into the end zone with little trouble. We were on the board as the quarter came to a close.

I was happy, but the thoughts kept nagging at me. After the play I had just made, *I* should have been the guy to take it in. *If* I was the tailback. *If I was the man.* But the Sundevils had two men and only one tailback.

I didn't like the way I was feeling. I wanted to be a team player. I liked Marcus, and I loved the games we played together. But I wanted to play the game for the rest of my life, not just for a couple of high school seasons, so I could sit around with these guys five years from now, drinking beer, and talking about that spin move I made back in the day.

This was my life, and I didn't feel good about its future. I couldn't remember ever being so torn on a football field. I said a little prayer that I might get past these notions and be able to uphold my role.

On the next set of downs...it happened. The call came in for an off-tackle play with Marcus. On the snap, I blew through the line and opened the hole with a solid block, but somebody's man wasn't blocked. He was trying to recover as Marcus hit the hole. The defender took his best chance and lunged toward Marcus just as he was high stepping over a fallen lineman. The guy's helmet smashed right into Marcus's knee, and he went down in agony. I was surprised, and for an instant, I didn't know what to do. Marcus was one of the toughest guys I knew. I thought he was indestructible.

I knelt down to see if he was all right; if it was serious. I felt relieved to see that he wasn't panicking. When there's a serious injury you can usually see it in the guy's eyes. Marcus had to have help to the sidelines. He would have to sit out a couple of series, that's all. The punt team took the field.

And then it hit me. I was the tailback. I tried not to think about it.

On the next possession, Coach called me over and said, "You're in at tail."

Cedrick, Marcus's brother, would come in at fullback. He was the kind of guy meant to play fullback. He was crazy, and he loved to hit people.

It was going to be the same "24 Power" play Marcus had just run. It felt funny lining up so far away from the line of scrimmage. I wanted to make sure I took the hand-off cleanly, since I would have more momentum than I usually had. Preston laid it in there just right. I saw Cedrick hit the line like a maniac. I hit the hole and I was gone. I broke it for 73 yards and my eleventh touchdown of the season. When I crossed the line I was screaming. I was pumped. It felt great.

But when I reached the sidelines I caught a glance at Marcus. Tears flowed from his eyes. As the doctor examined his knee I felt ashamed. Marcus didn't deserve this. He was the hardest working team player I had ever met. I could see it would be a long season and the thought of it filled me with mixed emotions.

Marcus managed to get back into the game and we went back to our usual formation. Nonetheless, I felt emotionally rattled. I lost my timing for the rest of the game.

26. REFLECTION

It's three o'clock in the morning.

How is it possible that I am so tired but still can't fall asleep? My body doesn't understand it either. It's just screaming at me. After all I demand of it, I don't even have the decency to allow it some rest? I lay there in a guilty heap.

If I fall asleep, my mind will be at the mercy of my conscience, and I don't feel like putting myself on trial. Not now. I'd rather stay awake, stuck in the same thoughts.

How did I get here? Where am I heading? How do I get there? The same thoughts spiral through my brain.

I think about my teammates, the coaches, Jay, Tom, Marcus, Preston, John, Moms.

I play conversations all night in my head, but they don't go anywhere. And they don't go away.

I talk to my dad. It's not a conversation. Just two men staring at each other. He finally shakes his head, chuckles a bit and walks through the old wooden door in his automotive garage, closing it behind him.

Just run the football, Showtime. Just run the football.

I try hard to believe it's that simple.

Family squabbles. Coaches with slick speeches and plastic smiles.

I look around my room, its furnishings and all the presents I've received.

All of them are gifts from the machine. I can't decide how much I've deserved and how much I've taken.

Just run the football.

Why isn't that enough?

I can see through the walls tonight. I look straight into the hearts of my roommates and relatives. I feel lost.

I peer into myself, then stop. I don't want to do that. Not right now. I have too many nice things all around me to look inside of myself.

I force my eyelids shut and tell my head to sink. Forget it. It's just me and the darkness tonight. The moon stays with me, though. It offers a little light and gives me a little comfort.

My eyes stay fixed on the moon. I am grateful. It's a small, necessary image, dependable until the sun rises and practice begins. Now I'm down to two thoughts, over and over: Just run the football, and, *why isn't that enough?*

27. MOVES

I needed to get back into my school work. I was doing everything I could to develop myself on the football field, but school was another matter. I honestly tried to concentrate on my studies, but the drama at Valley Prep always seemed to draw me away.

Don't get me wrong; I wasn't easily distracted. I knew, by this time, that if football took a bad turn I would need my education to fall back on. So, I stuck my butt in a classroom chair and kept it there.

John would swing by and say, "Hey, D, let's go to the mall and pick up some new CDs."

I was tempted. I wasn't really interested in the things we were studying, but most of the time I declined. "Nah, J," I said, "I got to get to class."

John respected my decision. He would go, of course, but that was John. He never felt guilty about anything.

Homework, papers and projects were hard for me that year. But suddenly, when I actually began going to class, the homework became easier. Funny, huh? It took me all that time to figure out that if I showed up and paid attention in class, it was easier to do the homework.

Other challenges presented themselves on the football field that began to draw my attention further away from my studies.

Marcus Wright-Fair was worse off than we all had thought and had to sit out at least a week to rest his knee. Just to show you the kind of team player he was, Marcus was out there all week in his practice grays, rooting us on and helping out where he could. I felt terrible about his injury, and Marcus knew it. He slapped me on the shoulder and said, "Go on and do what you gotta do, D." That was the kind of person he was.

I got to work, all right. I studied more film and put in more time getting the right jump off the snap and clean hand-offs from Preston. I even rolled over John Pearlman once or twice in the process. "You can't handle me, boy!" He was never too happy to hear this.

That week's game was a home game against Crespi Prep. It would be my first start at tailback and I was a little nervous. I called the offensive line together before the game and talked to them.

"Hey, you know Marcus is out, so let's pick it up this week. If you guys have a great game, I'll have a great game."

How did we do? The next morning's headline said it all:

SPARKS SCORES 6 TIMES AS VALLEY PREP ROLL

Tradition holds that a running back buys his offensive linemen dinner. However, Valley Prep's Derek Sparks should be giving the Crespi Prep defense that special treatment.

It was some night, and one thing in particular became clear to me. The difference in running from the tailback position was huge. Everything felt better, especially my increase in carries. I felt a rhythm throughout the game I hadn't felt before.

Every time I broke away on a running play, I glanced over to the sideline, and there was Marcus Wright-Fair, limping down the sideline cheering me on.

Meanwhile my six touchdowns and 215 yards had moved me into the CIF Southern Section lead in rushing, with 879 yards. Marcus was fifth in that category with 656 yards in just four games. But now we had the same number of carries for the first time. I was also first in scoring with 102 points on 17 touchdowns. Marcus was fifth with nine touchdowns. Our team offense ranked first, which was amazing for a team without a passing game. Our team defense was rated second. Our confidence soared.

Despite Marcus, and the example he had set, I still wondered how many yards and touchdowns I would have gained if I hadn't sat out the second half of most of the games we'd played.

The newspapers supported my thoughts. *The L.A. Times* wrote:

**SPARKS FLIES IN ROLE AS SUBSTITUTE TAILBACK:
DESPITE SITTING OUT MOST OF THE SECOND HALF,
THE VALLEY PREP JUNIOR SCORED SIX TOUCHDOWNS.**

In either the game's latter stages or it's aftermath, something occurred to Derek Sparks.

It might have been as he stood on the sidelines Friday night for most of the second half of his team's 55-14 walloping of Crespi Prep.

It might have been when he finally sat down and stared at the telling numbers on the statistics sheet.

Or it might have been Monday morning in class at Valley Prep.

"Man," he thought to himself, "I could've gained 500 yards. I could've scored 15 touchdowns."

To be sure, there is an element of hyperbole in these thoughts. There is, however, an element of reality too...

It dominated my thoughts. I was capitalizing on my friend's injury. It was a part of the game; but at the same time, he was going out of his way to support me. It just didn't seem right.

I was preoccupied with and consumed by my statistics. The issue weighed heavy on Jay and Tom as well. They put their differences behind them enough to agree that they should meet with the head coach together. Perspective and focus had flown out of the window. It was all about stats, hype and scholarships now.

Jay and Tom walked into Coach Santini's office and laid it out. They felt that I should have been the starting tailback. I had shown what I could do with the football when I was placed there and it was time for the coaches to come through on their promises. They'd promised to make me the star of the team. Jay expressed his thoughts in straight-forward terms. They left the coach sitting there, wondering what kind of a mess he had recruited himself into.

Well, join the club!

The next game against Southern was the beginning of a lot of drama at Valley Prep. Marcus was back after visiting the team "doctor," the same doctor John Pearlman was seeing. Whatever took place, sent Marcus back out, ready for action. His game stats were 117 yards rushing on just 9 carries.

With Marcus back in the game, we beat them so badly that the coaches agreed to keep the clock running and to reduce the length of the quarters, from twelve to eight minutes.

Marcus and I only played the first half. By the time we left the game, the score was 41-0. But the big news was that the coaches had created a platoon system, where Marcus and I would rotate at tailback.

He'd run a series of plays at tailback with me at fullback, then Cedrick Wright-Fair would come in at full and I would line up at tail. I was surprised to see it, but I sure wasn't going to complain. I had 166 yards on 12 carries, with touchdown runs of 7, 35, and 56 yards. I also connected on a 12-yard touchdown pass from Preston in the second quarter, bringing my touchdown total to 21 in 6 games.

Marcus's 117 yards included a 44-yard touchdown run. In regard to his 9 carries, the coaches told him that they were trying to bring him back slowly with his knee and all. But Marcus wasn't buying it.

◆◆◆

I don't remember a whole lot about the house we lived in while I was at Valley Prep, but I do remember that Tom's room—the converted family room—had a huge picture window.

I'll never forget looking out of that window the morning after the game with Southern and seeing Marcus and his dad walking to the coaches' office. Marcus's dad was a huge former pro football player. He had three sons at Valley Prep and was in no mood for double talk.

Mr. Wright-Fair lit into the coaches, reminding them that his son, who had served the team faithfully for three years, was the most sought after recruit in the country. He deserved the team's respect; he had earned his regular position and usual number of carries.

I don't know exactly what was said, but I do know that it went on for quite awhile and it wasn't a friendly meeting.

The coaches' drama was only beginning:

RUNNING FOR COVER:
VALLEY PREP FAILS TO WIN OVER ITS CRITICS
DESPITE UNBEATEN RECORD

The final gun sounded and Coach J.K. Santini, victorious again, headed to mid-field for the traditional post game handshake between coaches. Santini's Valley Prep had just defeated Crespi Prep 55-14.

Crespi Prep coach Mark Love was surly as he approached Santini. He felt that the Valley Prep coach was guilty of running up the score. Love was aware of the Sundevils reputation as a result of the 61-0 win over Bishop and a 37-0 upset over Sun Valley that has made Santini a less-than-popular figure among the coaching fraternity.

Last month, with a score of 42-7 in the first half, Coach Santini continued to play star running back Derek Sparks.

A 45-yard scoring run by the junior made the score 49-7 in the second quarter. That proved to be the final straw for Love.

As a result, what awaited Santini at mid-field was not so much a handshake as a take down.

"He was a little brusque, shall we say," Santini remembers.

And yet, when Santini turned around from the icy reception to head back and mingle with his coaches, friends and parents of players, he received little in the way of back slapping accolades.

Why in the world, parents wondered, did you pull Derek Sparks so early in the third quarter?

Why are you punishing him, making him sit out, just because the other team isn't as good as we are?

Santini was dumbfounded.

He had pulled Sparks early hoping to salvage his reputation and relationship with the coaching fraternity, only to hear from Love that it wasn't early enough. He then heard from parents that reducing the 17-year-olds playing time was also unfair.

He stood at San Gabriel College that night, a portrait in frustration. Behind him stood a snarling Love, a symbolic figure of the coaches Santini has alienated in just five games. In front of him stood the parents, symbolic figures of his players' aspirations.

"I can't win," Santini thought to himself. "I just can't win."

> *Like the traditional coin toss before each game, there were two sides to the Valley Prep football story. Each side has been tugging at Santini throughout the season, both were exhilarating and trying.*
>
> *The Sundevils and Santini, 38, stand in the eye of a storm. The Sundevils run up the score; opposing coaches cry. Their statistics and record are deceiving, the skeptics cry. The Sundevils play a bunch of cream puffs.*
>
> *In addition, critics accuse Valley Prep of recruiting its talent and bending rules to get athletes into school...*

Man, things really started to get deep after that. Not a moment passed without a parent, reporter or a CIF official storming onto campus and closing the door to the coaches' office.

None of us knew what was going down. All we could do was remain focused on the next upcoming game. But you reap what you sow, and all of us were going to have come to terms with reaping. Soon.

The situation was gnawing at Marcus Wright-Fair. He was hurt, but more by the coaches' lack of loyalty than by the platooning situation. Marcus was a smart guy, he knew the game, and he knew his way around a football field. He had his college career to think about. After all, he was one of the hottest football prospects in the country. Legal or not, Marcus had already had many intimate conversations with recruiters from several top-notch schools.

Marcus had been a team player and he expected the same courtesy from his coaches. He couldn't handle the way the coaches were pushing him aside without a decent explanation. But he knew why it was happening.

The coaches felt they had an unstoppable team with either one of us, so whom were they going to please? A senior who already had one foot out the door? No way.

They were going to make sure their junior star was happy, so they'd be sure that he returned next season. If, in the meantime, they found a younger player who was just as talented...Well, that returning senior was on his own. It was just that cut-throat.

Marcus went to the coaches. He tried to sit down and talk with them about what was happening. He had been their main guy for years. At a minimum, he thought, they owed him a frank discussion.

Maybe it was bad timing. The coaches were under the gun from ten different individuals, including my uncles, who were never easy to deal with.

Whatever the case, Marcus, with tears in his eyes, stood and pleaded before Santini and Hutchinson.

Do you know what they told him?

"If you're not happy here, maybe you should transfer."

Marcus lost it. He couldn't believe that after all the effort, pain and work he had given to the program, a transfer was the only option presented to him? He couldn't take it. He was finding out just how ruthless the machine could be.

He stayed with the team, but he was never the same guy. Sometimes he didn't even ride the team bus to games. He'd show up at the last minute, apathetic and completely aloof from the coaches. I didn't say a word.

◆◆◆

Another drama unfolded involving Preston. He felt cheated being made to play quarterback, when his future was as a receiver. He did his job, but gravely. The coaches always said, "Smile, Preston."

He answered blandly, "What's there to smile about?"

Preston, like Marcus, felt robbed of his due. Running game or no, he felt that he was a strong part of our team's offense and a stabilizing force in the backfield. But the media always kept its focus on Derek and Marcus, and whenever they mentioned Preston's name, it was the same old thing, "Derek's cousin, Preston Sparks…"

Besides that, Preston was kicking butt on defense. He was possibly the best free safety in the league. He had caught a slew of interceptions and not many quarterbacks could complete a pass while he was on the field. But ultimately, it was always "Derek, Derek, Derek," and Preston was sick of it.

All I could do was sympathize, and tell him, "It's not a fair game, Preston." It was easy for me to say, but my words didn't help him any.

Preston wanted out of all of this as soon as possible. He knew he could play college baseball just about anywhere. Probably football as well, but not at quarterback.

When Preston started reading articles about our games, he became irritated over the lack of coverage on his plays. When the press did mention him, they referred to him as "junior quarterback, Preston Sparks," even though he was a year older than me and had left Wharton in the middle of his junior year. He felt confused.

He kept seeing it, so he asked the coaches about it. They wouldn't give him straight answers, so he finally went to Jay and told him about the mistake.

"That's no mistake. They pushed you back a year so you'd have two years of eligibility," said Uncle Jay.

Preston couldn't believe it. He was a junior again? He couldn't take it. He wanted out of this school. But it was a done deal, and to raise a stink would bring attention to Valley Prep that no one wanted. He was stuck.

I think Preston also felt a little embarrassed. It tells you how seriously he was taking his classes, if, three months into the semester, he hadn't figured out what grade he was in. Now it would be one more year before he could get out from under the shadow of Derek Sparks.

I frequently found Preston brooding in his room, sometimes completely miserable, but he couldn't talk to me about it. How could he tell me that my celebrity status was eating away at him? He couldn't. Same as I couldn't tell him that it was my status that brought him here.

It wasn't a happy time at Valley Prep, but we kept on winning. To the coaches that was all that counted.

I tried to stay out of it, to keep my concentration pointed towards my studies and the game. Two-thirds of the way through the season I was posting good numbers. After seven games I was leading the CIF Southern Section in rushing with 1,314 yards on 129 carries (an average of over 10 yards per carry), and in scoring, 25 touchdowns.

Marcus Wright-Fair was right up there with me, although I wondered how, with his knee still injured. He was third in rushing with 1,103 yards, and fourth in scoring with 13 touchdowns.

We rolled through the rest of the regular season undefeated. Marcus had an 180 yard rushing game against L.A. Christian, and I gained 160 yards in our regular season closer, the toughest challenge of the year. Valley Prep took Eastern Christian 28-20.

Even though we felt engulfed in turmoil, we felt unbeatable on the football field. We were barreling into the playoffs behind a winning streak and a stockpile of dominating statistics.

28. Playoffs

The Valley Prep Sundevils entered the playoffs looking unbeatable. We were undefeated in the regular season and our defense had surrendered a mere 70 points. We were rolling. We had the league's number one and number three rushers, and I ended the regular season second in California in points scored. I had scored 186 points on 31 touchdowns.

We looked and felt like a powerhouse.

Forget that six of our blue chip players had been illegally recruited, or that a number of our players were using steroids.

Forget that Valley Prep had players on the field who were academically ineligible.

Forget that we had money in our pockets that didn't belong there.

All that mattered was the game, and we were winning.

The game. Most of us at Valley Prep were playing a couple of them. We played the game by a different set of rules, using a distorted set of values.

Our focus was on winning the championship. That was the only game we were playing. We wanted to grasp that trophy to see where else it might lead.

Now we were in the spotlight; the players, the coaches, my uncles, and me. While enjoying all the attention, I think that we all saw storm clouds rolling in too.

◆◆◆

Our first round playoff opponent was Dorsey High. They were a good team, with a strong kickoff returnee named Taro Spikes who managed to hurt us on a couple good returns. They shut us out in the first quarter, and we left the field at half-time, tied 7-7.

When we returned for the third quarter, Dorsey High continued to play us tough, scoring with three minutes left in the third, and tying the game again, 14-14.

I received the kickoff, took the ball at the 6-yard line, and was never touched. A 94 yard touchdown run.

On the next set of downs our defense shut them down completely, three downs and out.

On the following series, Marcus Wright-Fair went off the right side for 65 yards and another touchdown. That was it. We won 28-14. Marcus had a monster game, rushing for 205 yards and three touchdowns to dwarf my gain of 121 yards.

We expected an even bigger challenge in the second round, but we never let Silmore High get close. We blew them out 35-8. We had earned a reputation for trash talking and lived up to it on this night.

We celebrated long and hard after that one. We were on our way to the semifinals and had never felt stronger.

Our opponent was a team from a small town nobody had ever heard of. Cascade was their name and we wondered how they had even reached the semis. We knew that the teams we would face on the road to the finals would be tough match ups, but Cascade wasn't in our class.

Our week of practice was light; the coaches wanted us to reserve our energy for the finals in two weeks.

We were loose and relaxed on the bus ride to the game. John led the party. I was deep into my music, but I sensed how confident the players were. It was a long bus-ride to the football stadium in the mountains and the cold thin mountain air.

Most guys kept moaning, "Man, lets get this over with quick and get the hell back to civilization."

It was over quickly. Before we knew it, Cascade had upset us 7-0. It was a nightmare. We embarrassed ourselves at every turn. We had lost. Our dreams of the finals would remain just that. After the game we sat on the field and cried.

People have a lot of theories about why it happened. Lots of excuses. But to me, we just lost. We lost because we took the game too lightly. We thought we were unbeatable, but we weren't. We were playing on the road in the freezing cold and we couldn't handle it. We were unaccustomed to the thin air and we fatigued well before they did.

In our own little corner of the world we were repeating history's classic mistake. We strutted through the season with an arrogance begging to be humbled. That day, we were humbled.

The machine had failed. We had been out-coached. Our coaches had led us into the lion's den. We were unprepared and riding on our past successes. We had dominated every game by using the same couple of running plays over and over. Since our running backs were so talented, the strategy had always worked, but we became predictable.

Cascade had scrutinized our game films and had developed a much more sophisticated game plan than our coaches' five-play playbook.

Cascade didn't even pretend that we might pass the ball. A normal defense keeps at least four defensive players back to defend against the pass or a breakaway run. Not Cascade. It seemed like they blitzed everybody on every play.

They were in a "4-4" defense all night, four linebackers and four defensive linemen. We called it "Eight In The Box." The whole team, except for three defensive backs, charged in at the snap, blitzing Preston and clogging up every last running lane.

They must have sacked Preston a million times. When Marcus or I got the ball, we had nowhere to go. Just a wall of Cascade uniforms hungry to collapse on us. We had no pass plays to count on or to keep them honest.

As the game wore on, we grew tired, but the tenacious Cascade defense never ceased. We were whipped. All they needed to win was their lone touchdown.

Even today it's hard for me to discuss it. They should have burned the film. I wish I could burn the memory.

29. IMAGE

Numb.

That's how I felt after my first season at Valley Prep. We had won a lot of games (12-1) and I had posted some impressive numbers (1,944 yards rushing, 35 touchdowns). Still, I felt numb. It wasn't a bad feeling. It wasn't a good feeling either.

A lot of great things happened on the field. A lot of awards poured in as a result. But it all felt tainted.

I led the CIF Southern Section in rushing and scoring, and was named to the All-CIF Southern Section Team. I was the *Los Angeles Times* Running Back of the Year. I was listed as the hottest college recruiting prospect in the country and was invited to several prestigious sports banquets.

Awards kept coming in, one after the other. The Los Angeles Times presented me with a trophy nearly identical to the Heisman trophies I had seen in USC's Heritage Hall. College recruiters clogged my telephone line. I began screening my calls. The college recruiters who couldn't get through, flooded me with mail.

The *Los Angeles Times* reported:

> *Derek Sparks' success on the football field has kept the postal carrier busy in his neighborhood.*

And...

> *Derek Sparks gazes proudly at a basket overflowing with letters from some of the nation's most recognizable universities: USC, Notre Dame, UCLA, Florida, Michigan. All promise the Valley Prep running back the good life as a college football star.*
>
> *But the correspondence represents more to Sparks than just the prospect of a college scholarship. It proves that his California dream has been fulfilled and symbolizes the reason he left his small-town home in Texas two years ago. No high school record in the state is safe this year, not even Russell White's.*

Anyone who knew anything about high school sports knew that Russell White was related to the USC Heisman trophy winner, Charles White.

With my football career going strong, I needed a break.

I knew that I needed to begin studying for the SAT again. Reality hit me in the jaw. I wanted to get it taken care of, but I knew I wasn't ready. Just thinking about it depressed me. I sure had my work cut out.

John popped in and saw me slumped on the couch, moping. "What's up with you?" he inquired cheerfully. "You look like you just lost the CIF semi-finals or something."

"That's not funny, J," I said.

"Yeah, I know," John agreed. "For real, what's wrong with you?"

"Aw, I'm trying to get myself up to study for this SAT."

"Derek," he said, "why are you wasting your time studying for that stupid test?"

"It ain't stupid, John. I need that score for college."

"Yeah, I know that. But, you know, it's not like you're one of those book worm types that do well on those kinds of tests. You know they say those tests are racially biased, and they damn sure are biased against athletes." He laughed. "It ain't fair. So, why should you have to study for it?"

He caught me at a low point. His logic almost made sense to me. I wanted it to make sense. "What am I gonna do?"

"Derek, for one time, just this once, listen to me. You're tired and you need a break. Go home to Texas, see your family for Christmas. Let me take care of the SAT. Nobody needs to know. Jay, Tom, none of 'em. Besides, this is how it's done for star athletes. I know you like to play things by the book, but this'll be on me. Just go and try not to think about it."

I did just that. And, I tried not to think about it.

Preston and I packed up for a two week visit to Wharton. I had a lot of mixed emotions about leaving California, but I really wanted to see my family. My mom, my cousins, everyone.

The principal, Pop Wilson, dropped by, as we were loading the car for the airport. He had been giving out T-shirts to all of the players as Christmas gifts. He gave Preston and me an entire box of merchandise. Poking out the corner of each box was a single blank white envelope.

"Christmas cards," he explained with a wink.

What he said next, I remember like it was yesterday.

"Have a good time in Texas, but make sure you boys come back."

I felt confused. Why would he worry about us coming back? We shook hands and got into the car. We kept our envelopes sealed until we were on our way to the airport.

Each envelope held two one-hundred dollar bills. Merry Christmas.

Wharton hadn't changed a bit, but it sure felt different. It was surprising how much I had adjusted to Los Angeles. Wharton felt so much smaller and poorer than I had remembered.

It was really good to be back in my mom's place. Eating good ol' soul food: greens, corn bread, fried chicken, candied yams...and you talk about pies! I had never eaten so much homemade pie in all my life. I almost O.D.'d.

All my little cousins had grown. They spent the entire weekend asking me for tips about the game of football. It was fun and I felt like a role model.

I remember all of us sitting and talking for hours. Everyone wanted to hear stories about Los Angeles. My whole family sat there with their mouths hanging open.

I told them about the TV sitcom stars we had on campus, and kids whose parents were producers and directors in the movie and music industries. They couldn't believe the stories I was telling them, as they fell into moods of awe, almost fear. They couldn't imagine this small-town kid around all of those big-time people.

When I was finally able to sit quietly with Mom there wasn't much to say. I never considered it before, but we had never talked much. We were finally able to sit down like two adults and have a conversation for the first time in years, but neither one of us had the words. So, we just sat together, and that was all right.

I ran into Buckwheat—Dante Dickerson—from across the street. He was doing well, still wiping his nose on his sleeve. He was playing football for the high school and having a good time. We joked about him coming out to California to play, but I knew his folks wouldn't go for that. He knew it too. He was a Texas boy at heart.

No matter how old I get, I know I can come home to Wharton, and Buckwheat will still be there, wiping his nose on his sleeve.

That night, my five-year-old cousin handed me one of his story books. I enjoyed reading to him.

I was reading "Hansel and Gretel," the story about two kids who wander off in the forest until they reach a magical place of candy and gingerbread. They can't resist eating everything in sight and begin to think they've discovered the greatest place in the world. Only later do they discover it's all a trap. The wicked witch, an evil force, was just trying to fatten them to flavor her soup.

The more I read, the sadder I felt. I wanted to tell my little cousin to watch out. High school athletics can be like that gingerbread house. Everybody makes you think you can eat all you want, that it's all candy. Meanwhile, you get fatter and fatter, thinking you have it made. In the end, they're just making soup.

Some bedtime story.

I ran into Omar and was glad to see him. We hugged. When I looked into his eyes I saw that he was high on something. I didn't know what it was. I didn't want to know. But it was great just to sit and talk. He was still playing football, still the best in Wharton. He was going on about how he was going to see me at the college level, on the same field. I took him by the arm and spoke from the heart.

"Uncle Jay wants you to give him a call about coming back to California," I said. "He can set you up. You'll be living with Preston and me. It'll be better than home!"

"Nah, thanks though." He smiled but I saw a little wisp of sadness cross his face.

"Why not, man? You're the greatest running back in Texas. Can you imagine the damage you could do in California? You gotta do it, man. It's not too late."

He shrugged. "Thanks, man, I appreciate it, but I got things goin' on here, you know?"

"What? You need to get out of this place, Omar. You need to..."

He grabbed me by the shirt to stop me. He pulled me closer to him. His eyes were even glassier up close. And red.

"California ain't for me, D. You always had a plan. That's good; I know you're gonna make it. I wasn't cut out for all that, you understand?"

I didn't understand.

My last stop was to see my father. He looked the same. He talked about how I had filled out. I told him I was playing at a private school in San Gabriel, California. He looked at me like he was trying to decide whether to believe me or not. Then he shrugged and took a puff off his cigar. Conversation was still awkward; he was still my father.

"I'm gonna come out and see you play." I knew he wasn't. He knew that he wasn't. I wanted to tell him how many yards I had gained, how many touchdowns I had scored, that I was State Sophomore Player of the Year. All of it. I knew he didn't care.

"I'll send you some tickets," I said, and got up to leave. He gave me an absent nod.

Wharton was simple, but it wasn't my home. Not anymore. I had a complicated extended family now, waiting for me back in California.

I had family members angling for the cash, rationalizing their behavior as some kind of good cause. Jay and Tom were ready to clobber each other, all in the name of my best interests.

I had Coach Santini, Hutchinson and Pop Wilson there for me; but, of course, that all hinged on my ability to run the football. They were, after all, really there for the money, power and championships.

I had some homies, my teammates, juicing up on steroids, and most pocketing the perks of the game without a second thought.

Like the rest of my extended family, I too, had my hands deep into the pockets of the machine.

It was all a part of the game and things couldn't have been less clear.

"I love you Mom," I said, boarding the plane back to Los Angeles. "Here's two hundred bucks."

30. HOME

On the flight back to California, a million thoughts spun around in my head. Too much had happened in such a short time. I just stared out of the window, thinking.

During the vacation Uncle Jay called me in Wharton a number of times. He sounded worked up and it made me nervous. He told me that he had been butting heads with the coaches on a regular basis. They were at the point where they simply wouldn't talk to him. They said he was too volatile. They didn't want to deal with him. Jay suspected that they were up to something else.

I knew there was more to the story than what he was telling me.

Jay maintained that promises were not kept. Right or wrong, Jay's word was good and he expected the same from others.

The longer he talked, the louder he became.

"Valley Prep better come through with what they promised. The Texas Connection is gonna get rollin'. You are gonna be the full time tailback. Preston's gonna get his opportunity. All of it...or I'll pull you all out of there."

His speech was rapid, breathless, angry. "You...Preston...I'll even take your boy John and that Leon too. We'll move to a school that'll give us what we need...What we deserve!"

I didn't like the sound of that 'we' thing. Everything seemed to be about deals and what everybody could get. I was getting real nervous. I didn't like being someone's poker chip. It hurt me to be my uncle's poker chip.

Jay went on. "If they think they can just shut me out, they got another thing coming."

Where in the conversation had the *we* turned into *he*?

"When you get back to school we're gonna lay it on the line. They're gonna listen to what I have to say or we're moving on.

"Shoot, if they had any good sense at all, you all would be state champions right now. But these no-coaching so-and-so's are so busy counting how many carries Marcus Wright-Fair has and how many Derek has, they don't even know what's going on, on the field!"

I fidgeted in my seat throughout the flight, trying to digest and sort it all out. I didn't want to move to another school just because Jay was angry with the coaching staff. Last season had been a disappointment, but I was ready to move on to the next season.

After all, I had what I needed. I was going to be the tailback. Marcus's graduation settled that matter. Last season's back-up quarterback, Eddie Stuart, was giving hope to the coaches' plans for a passing game. Preston could return next season as a receiver. I was happy with the house on campus and with my expectations on the field. I felt excited about the direction in which I was heading.

Education, school, classes? What priority does a group of unsupervised teenagers put on books and classes when they have a room full of toys—CD's, big-screen TVs—and pockets full of Pop Wilson's cash? We gave school as much thought as we gave the acceptance of gifts.

When we arrived back on campus, Valley Prep had a surprise for us. It was decided that the school needed to build more classrooms and the house we were living in would have to be torn down. I couldn't believe it. The coaches and the principal told me not to worry. They would work something out with an apartment owner nearby.

Jay went off. If they thought he was crazy before, he really showed his behind this time. The battles were loud and vicious, and I couldn't stand to be around any of them.

I started hanging out at John Pearlman's house in Grant Hills. It was quiet there, and his mom, Susie, and stepfather, Ron, seemed like nice people.

There I could avoid Jay's endless angry calls telling me what we were going to do to Valley Prep and what other school he was looking into.

The coaches weren't letting up either. They said that my uncle was a maniac and unstable. They threw a ton of insults at him.

Recruiters called day and night. Reporters beeped in on call-waiting to find out the inside scoop. It was all too much. It was more than I could take.

Jay gave the apartment proposal a quick, flat rejection. He told them that we had refused a similar deal at Central. If we had liked it, we would have stayed there. Jay wanted the house. The house Pop Wilson had promised for the Texas Connection. Jay was adamant. He claimed it was his due.

I felt my schoolwork slipping away from me. But now Jay was calling John and me, telling us not to go to school. He said that it was the only way to show them we were serious.

So I stayed out of a school for a couple of days. Was it a mistake? Huge! But this was my father, or at least as close to one as I was going to have, instructing me to follow *his* orders. He had brought me here. He had taken care of a lot of other people within my family, and me too. Pulling out his parental clout, Jay was putting the potential of *his* Texas Connection above everything else, including my wishes. Jay gave the order; I went along.

Recruiters were showing up, anxious. "Is everything okay? Are you staying at Valley Prep? Are you out?"

Bernardi, the coach from USC, became really concerned. That frightened me. I had a path all laid out to the Coliseum, but now I felt like I was being shoved back to where I began.

I envisioned all of the schools getting scared away, one after the other. What college or university would put itself in the middle of this mess?

Finally, John asked if I wanted to stay with his family until things were straightened out. They really liked me. Saying that it would be no problem, they invited Tom and Preston to stay there as well. But those guys were into their freedom and their privacy. They wanted to party.

So I moved in with the Pearlmans and the coaches thoroughly approved. Of course they would have approved of any situation that excluded Jay.

Jay was watching his whole plan unravel. Without me he'd lose his leverage. I just wanted the whole thing to pass. Go to school and play football, that's all I wanted.

Jay came and met the Pearlmans. He could see that they were good people who didn't understand the campus politics. So he tried to explain what was happening, impressing on them how the school had mistreated him. He probably gave up too much information. They probably didn't care.

The Pearlmans didn't see how the issues Jay was ranting and raving about had anything to do with my education or me. That was their bottom line.

Coach Santini called the next day to express his concern. He wanted to know why I wasn't in school, and warned me that my Uncle Jay was crazy, irrational and dangerous.

The Pearlmans must have felt like they were walking on a tightrope.

I felt torn. This was my uncle they were talking about. I loved him and was grateful to him for all he had done. But he was beginning to look a little crazy to me as well. It was awful. The walls were closing in and I couldn't find any escape.

The Pearlmans wanted to know what I was going to do about school.

I went back to class.

When Jay found out he felt hurt and mad as hell. He raced out to the Pearlmans. He screamed at me and said that I was allowing the coaches and the Pearlmans to brainwash me.

I screamed back. "The Pearlmans are concerned about my education. They are encouraging me to do well in school. That was your first priority too; wasn't it Uncle Jay? Remember? What happened to all of that?

"I'll tell you what happened. The Texas Connection ran right over it."

Then he snapped.

"That's it. After all I've done for you, you stand up in my face and try to accuse me of something like this? I don't believe it. Fine. If the Pearlmans know so much, if the Pearlmans are your family, then fine! You let the Pearlmans deal with all of this bull crap! I'm out of here!" Then, he left.

Lower, lower, lower. I walked around like a zombie.

Tom and Preston had worked out a deal with the school regarding their housing. One of our teammate's, Steve Cebrian, said that his parents had just separated. His mother was willing to share her emancipated mansion with the boys.

Okay, Steve was a rich kid, but his lifestyle made Tom and Preston look like the pope. It made me uncomfortable just visiting them. I wanted no part of that atmosphere. Every time I saw Preston, I wondered which leg his mother would break first if she knew what was going on behind those huge security gates.

It was a bad time. I was looking for somebody to give me some peace of mind. The Pearlmans were great people, but they didn't know what was going on in my head.

That's when the coaches stepped in. They must have had radar. It was just the right time for them to say all the things I needed to hear to erase my apprehensions.

They told me I was a good kid with a future. A future Jay could ruin. They came to the Pearlman's house, explaining that they just wanted to make sure I was all right. They reiterated my importance to the team. They gave me some money, and told Susie that if I needed anything, anything at all, all she had to do was call.

Susie wanted to know who was responsible for me. Who should she call if I got sick or hurt? Who was in charge?

The coaches shook their heads and preached some more about what a bad guy Jay was, how he had walked out on his responsibility. But they told her not to worry. "We'll take care of it," they said.

My life moved from bad dreams to nightmares when, not long after that conversation, Coach Hutchinson told Susie that the school had figured out a way I could be properly taken care of. There was just one problem. I needed a legal guardian, one with my best interest at heart.

They laid it on the line. Would the Pearlmans be willing to become my legal guardian, to help protect my future? When put like that, the Pearlmans felt compelled to answer yes.

Hutchinson explained the deal. A friend of the program, a guy named Bombech, at the San Gabriel office of the Juvenile Corrections Department, could work it out so the government would pay for my clothes and housing. All the Pearlmans would have to do was to sign on as my legal guardians. Simple. Jay had walked out and somebody needed to step in, they reasoned. The Pearlmans were fine with the arrangement.

Hutchinson's friend, Bombech, must have held a high position within the Corrections Department. A couple of days later we all went to some court building. I meet with an attorney who introduced himself as a friend of the program. He asked me if I understood I'd be living with the Pearlmans and that they would assume my guardianship. I said I understood. The Pearlmans signed some papers and that was it. The coaches became elated. I just felt relief.

The Pearlmans got to work right away building a twenty thousand dollar room addition onto their home. I felt excited and scared at the same time. I mean, how much of it was because of Valley Prep's influence? Or, did the Pearlmans care twenty thousand dollars worth for a kid like me?

I feared what would happen if Jay ever found out about all this. But after I saw the plans and blueprints for my room—the walk-in closet, bathroom

*The Pearlmans
got busy right
away adding
on a room
for me.*

spa and separate entrance to the heated pool—I put all of my fears to rest.

Susie took me out to buy new school clothes. For the first time in a while, I felt like I was part of a family again. I thought maybe things would finally begin to settle. That's just when I received a frantic phone call from Jay.

"What the hell is going on? What's this about you being adopted?"

I tried to explain what was going on. But Jay had more to say.

"What is this about you being arrested?"

"Arrested?"

"So you've been *adopted* because you were *abandoned.*"

I didn't know what he was talking about.

When Jay explained it, I thought I was hearing a "B" movie script. The coaches had Bombech dummy up a phony arrest report, allowing them to go to the juvenile courts and claim that I'd been arrested as an abandoned runaway. To prevent this troubled, abandoned kid from further wrongdoing, the court should award legal custody to this nice domesticated white family in the hills.

The only reason Jay, or anyone else found out about it, was because of a technical mistake made by the Corrections Department. Someone had accidentally sent copies of the paperwork to my grandmother's home in Texas.

I could only imagine what kind of phone call occurred between my mom and Jay when she opened that letter explaining that her son, her only child, had been abandoned, arrested, and adopted!

"Send him home!" she screamed.

What could Jay say? This was the first time he had heard of it. He hung up, furious.

The newspapers got a hold of the story and my life turned upside down. I didn't know what to do and neither did the Pearlmans. The coaches told everybody to relax, not to overreact.

"Everything would have been fine," said Coach Hutchinson, "if that madman, Jay, hadn't leaked the story to the press."

I didn't know what to think, but I knew this latest scandal was going to ruin my reputation. The media was running wild with the story:

EX-CENTRAL PLAYER FINDS A HOME AT VALLEY PREP

Derek Sparks gazes proudly at a basket overflowing with letters from some of the nation's most recognizable universities, USC, Notre Dame, UCLA, Michigan. All promise the Valley Prep running back the good life as a college football star.

...Caught in a battle with Jay Sparks, his uncle and former legal guardian, Derek sought refuge in L.A. County juvenile court claiming he had been abandoned. The court assumed legal custody and Sparks is now a foster child of Ron and Susie Pearlman, whose son John is a teammate of Sparks at Valley Prep.

Jay Sparks and mother, June Sparks, who lives in Texas, object to the arrangement and want Derek to leave the Pearlman's Grant Hills home and move into an apartment with his cousin Preston, a proposal neither Derek nor Preston favor.

Preston lives with the Cebrian family, whose son Steven played defensive back for the Sundevils last season.

Jay Sparks strenuously denies that he abandoned Derek and claims that Valley Prep, and friends of the program, have plotted to gain control of his nephew. His suspicions began in January and climaxed when he learned that he had lost legal guardianship of Derek to the court.

"I was like a grizzly bear, and someone had come and taken my cub," the elder Sparks said. "I couldn't believe they were saying that I abandoned him. No way. I still say they cooked the whole thing up to get me out of the picture, so they can control Derek's future."

(Valley Prep coach) J.K. Santini, the Pearlmans, and Derek Sparks all deny that. Derek says he is happy living with the Pearlmans and wants to stay there, but is pained because his uncle and his mother wish otherwise.

"I don't know why your own people would put pressure on you when you're trying to perform your best," he said. "This is all hurting me. I'm busting my butt every day to do things right so I won't have criticism coming at me in all these directions. It's getting to the point where the football field is the only place I can have some peace..."

Too much so, as far as Jay Sparks was concerned. When he gained little satisfaction after voicing his concerns to Santini, the football coach, and principal Pop Wilson, he threatened to withdraw Derek from school.

"After I told them we were looking for a new school, they started to hate me," he said. "That's when they cooked up this whole thing. They got him conditioned to talk to me in a certain way. Derek was being used, and he didn't know it."

Jay Sparks claims that his fears were confirmed when the Pearlmans became Derek's foster parents.

Derek and the Pearlmans offer a totally different version of events. They claim that Jay lost touch with Derek for more than a month last winter, prompting Derek to suggest the idea of foster care.

"That's when everyone blew their top and started tripping out," Derek said about his family. "I like to went crazy over that. I felt like I was about to explode."

Said Ron Pearlman, "After everything was done, then I found out that his family was upset. I should have gone to his family first. I'm not trying to take anyone's family away..."

I felt awful. I didn't want Jay to feel the way he did. I had tried to do what was best for me and it was evolving into a monstrous mess.

I couldn't call Jay. I knew he wouldn't take the call. I called a local sports reporter who had written several articles about me.

"I need to put something in the newspaper," I said. He published this letter that appeared in the *Times* Sports section.

ROLANDO OTERO / for The Times

Derek Sparks has been the target of recruiting pitches from such prominent schools as USC, Notre Dame, UCLA and Michigan.

SPARKS LAUDS UNCLE, FOSTER FAMILY AFTER STORY APPEARS

I want to clarify some issues regarding me, my uncle Jay, cousin Preston and the Pearlman family.

I don't feel abandoned by Jay. He is the reason why I'm here in California. He came to my rescue when I was in the projects in Texas. He filled the shoes of my father and that's why I look up to him.

In my eyes he's still my legal guardian. If I had a problem, I'd go to him first. I love him the same way I did from day one at Central High.

The Pearlmans are good people and I'm anxious for this thing to be resolved so that my family and outsiders can see that they're not the bad people that they are reported to be. They're down-to-earth human beings and their intentions are good. I'm very appreciative of the things they've done for me. I'm living with them because I asked them to. The arrangement was okayed by my uncle, Jay Sparks.

Jay has not lost control of me. I'm not brainwashed by anyone. I know where I'm headed. I do trust my family. If Jay wants to reunite Preston and me under one roof, consider it done.

I have to start concentrating on football. As the top running back prospects in the country, I have goals and expectations to fulfill. I want this to be the last time I talk about these issues.

Thank you.

Derek Sparks,

Valley Prep running back

I hoped the letter would satisfy Jay enough to let us all move forward. The article seemed to work. Jay talked with the Pearlmans and I decided to stay with them.

Jay didn't fight me, but he was still a long way from happy. I just wanted to get my mind back on football and the coming senior season. I didn't know that the roller coaster ride was only beginning.

It was tougher being #1
than trying to become #1.
No one was happy,
least of all me.

31. DESCENT

The season looked promising to everyone at Valley Prep. The machine was greased and all parts were running smoothly. Eighteen starters were returning from the previous season and some roster moves were made to plug up the gaps that had weakened us during the previous season. Hot new recruits were arriving on campus every week.

Eddie Stuart, the backup quarterback, had spent the entire off-season with the track team, improving on his speed and running skills. That gave him some mobility to go with a competent throwing arm. Now Eddie had the makings of a decent quarterback.

This was the best news in the world for Preston. It freed him from his agony at the quarterback position, and allowed him to switch over to receiver.

He made it clear to the coaches that he wouldn't return to the team as a quarterback. He would rather have gone on and graduated. UCLA had offered him a scholarship. The MVP honor at the Terry Donahue football camp had all but ensured him of a full ride. But the Valley Prep coaching staff wanted their championship, and if it meant tacking on a fifth year to Preston's eligibility, so be it. Preston would just have to be content spending another year at Valley Prep.

Marcus Wright-Fair signed a letter of intent to USC. He was not only next in line to become the Trojan tailback, but was offered the opportunity to start as a true freshman at fullback. Marcus chose to remain second string at his better position. Either way it was great news.

Cedrick, who was mainly known as Marcus's little brother, turned out to be the older brother. He graduated with Marcus. He was a year older, but pushed back a year by the Valley Prep coaches. He was just one of a group of players who graduated after a fifth year of eligibility. I didn't understand how Valley Prep could pull it off, but they did, constantly.

Their graduation opened the door for Ray Jackson—the linebacker John had knocked unconscious the year before—to step in as the starting fullback. No one doubted Ray's potential.

John Pearlman became both the starting middle linebacker and the starting tight end. His size, recklessness and anger continued to grow. He couldn't get to our opening game fast enough.

Leon Lett was not only returning, he was returning as one of the top lineman prospects in the country. He had elevated his game and was ready to do some serious damage. If only he could pick up his mess!

With Marcus at USC, the tailback position was mine. The newspapers were already creating murmurs, citing my potential to break the all-time rushing record in California. I was hungry for the challenge. Thinking of carrying the football at tailback for an entire season only steeled my confidence. Even with so many emotional distractions, I was in the zone, ready to compete.

Yet, the media was ruthless. They didn't care what zone I was in; on any given day reporters stayed ready to pounce on me in the locker room, on the field, or between my classes.

They even had a standard method of interrogation: Was I speaking to Jay? How much money did the Pearlmans receive from the state of California for my child care? (I think it was something like five hundred dollars a month. I could eat that much in groceries in a single week.) Would my abandonment affect my performance? What chance did I have of toppling Russell White's career rushing record of 5,998 yards? The questions came in a constant, irritating barrage.

I tried to be as polite as I could to the media. Jay had always told me, "You can do these interviews as much as you want. Just be careful. Think before you speak."

It was all but impossible for me to anticipate my answers to reporters when I knew that their sole motivation was to twist my words and cajole me into saying anything remotely controversial. They wanted to hear me say that Jay was wrong or crazy.

I tried again and again to explain that Jay was my family. Most people didn't understand him, but I did. A family does what it has to do. Sometimes there are disagreements, but you stick it out and stay together. At least, that's the belief I held then. My family was my bedrock. I always considered our relationships and loyalties to each other to be beyond reproach.

I understood that the reporters were just trying to do their jobs. They had families to feed. But it didn't seem right to come after a 16-year-old kid they knew to be under a mountain of pressure, with their badgering and fast-talking for a piece of dirt or a juicy quotation.

How their articles affected my future was of no consequence to them. Every suggestion they printed, labeling me as a troubled, difficult kid with a crazy, greedy family, would have to be explained. I was fully accountable for every quotation but no one gave me any chance to respond.

I was getting phone calls from Texas every day. One day Moms called. Another day Grandma or Grandpa or one of my aunts was burning up the phone lines. There was a lot of crying on the phone, and screaming. Everyone wanted to know what was the matter with me, why was I was disobeying Jay? Why was I living with these people instead of with my own family?

I understood their frustration, but I also knew they had only heard one side of this huge soap opera. They didn't have all the facts.

The Pearlmans were like my second family. I was an outsider, but they welcomed me into their home as if I was one of their own. Except for my mom, the Pearlmans were as loving to me as any blood relative had ever been.

Susie, John's mother, was as loving to me as any blood relative had ever been.

I received stacks of letters every day from colleges, touting their schools and their athletic programs. Recruiters lurked around campus—three to five men every day, neatly dressed in polo shirts, cotton slacks, and their respective school colors—looking for a moment alone to throw their sales pitches at me.

One might wear a university hat, another might carry a briefcase, but the uniform was consistent, as was what they offered; opportunity. Don't get me wrong, to me this was like a dream coming true; but, man, it was distracting! I couldn't imagine worse timing.

The coaches never missed a chance to throw me a curve. I became their appointed ambassador, showing the campus to some hot new prospects. Guys like Ontiwan Carter and Keyshawn Johnson. That was just to remind me that my position was never safe.

If you don't know who these guys are, just open up any sports section. Ontiwan was the most highly publicized running back since...well, since me. He had dominated defenses with every carry. He went on to star at the University of Arizona.

Keyshawn, a phenomenal receiver from Dorsey High, ended up at USC, rewrote the school's record books and later became the first pick in the NFL draft. Neither one enrolled at Valley Prep, which was probably lucky for me. Two fewer things to worry about.

The biggest distraction of all came in the mail. I had all but forgotten about my arrangement with John to take care of my SAT score. I hadn't thought about it for a while, but I knew that if Jay ever caught wind of my deal with John, there would be hell to pay.

When I received my SAT results, tearing open the envelope, I thought it was a practical joke. John was fooling around, pulling a gag on me. I couldn't believe my eyes. Whoever John had persuaded to fake my identification and take the test for me had received a nearly perfect score!

John thought it was no big deal, but it was a very big deal. It was trouble. There was no way anyone would believe that I had raised my score nearly one thousand points, in just a matter of months. I was scared stiff.

Sure enough, a letter arrived a week later. Questions arose regarding the authenticity of my scores. I could either come in for an evaluation or retake the test. There wasn't much of a choice. I would study my butt off and retake the test.

The coaches, knowing that I was under a lot of pressure, had a peculiar way of dealing with it. They added more.

They called me in for a talk.

"Now Derek, I hope you see what kind of opportunity you've got here," said Coach Hutchinson. "Everything is riding on this season. You've got to fly."

I wondered what he meant by "everything." It would soon be clear.

"We'll be playing tougher teams; teams that have been studying game film on you all summer long, just waiting to knock you off," said Hutchinson. "Now that you won't have Marcus here to take the pressure off of you, you can't let that happen. You can't let down. If Valley Prep has another big season, I'm positive that I can land us all at USC or UCLA."

Us?

"You and Preston will play ball at the university and I will come along as a coach or recruiter, or maybe your personal mentor. I'll be there to look out for the two of you."

So, that was the angle. Coach would deliver two All-American players and land a college position for himself. They *needed* me to have a big season and they didn't want any interference from Jay.

I didn't bat an eye. This was just one more ridiculous issue in an already insane situation. I let the conversation roll off my back. I just jogged out to the field for practice.

32. HAWAII

Our first pre-season game was an invitational in Hawaii. I was as ready as I would ever be. Our league, the WAC, was moved to Division X, where we were ranked number one in the pre-season polls. The poor quality of the division, though, made many people question our invitation. The event organizer, when asked why Valley Prep had been invited, responded, "We want to see Derek Sparks play."

It was a miracle that I ever set foot in Hawaii. Jay was against Preston and me going. He continued to demand our transfer from Valley Prep.

I tried my best to explain to him that I couldn't handle another transfer. I'd have to adjust to a new team, leave all of my friends behind; and I knew that negative publicity would hurt my standing with college recruiters.

Jay said that he understood, but he warned me that the situation at Valley Prep would only get worse.

"They think they've got you now," he said. "You wait and see, they'll dog you in the end. They don't give a damn about what's best for you and they damned sure don't know how to keep their promises. Not to you, not to Preston, not to me. They'll use you, take everything they can get from you and then leave you hangin' in the wind. You watch."

It was hard for me to digest the things he was saying. Jay was truly committed to his "conspiracy theory" and had taken a beating in the papers for it. He genuinely felt that the coaches had plotted to push him out so they could control Preston and me without making good on their promises to him.

At the time, I had trouble buying into it. I knew my coaches weren't the type to follow the rules, but I couldn't believe the whole notion of a conspiracy. I reasoned, what would someone gain from that?

I tried to reassure Jay that I could handle it, that everything would work out. I tried to get him excited about how the team was developing, but he didn't want to hear a word of it.

In the end, we both knew that the decision would have to come from me. Jay had taught me to take responsibility for my life, ever since that first afternoon outside the Central High School gates.

"Forward or backward?" he said that day. I'd been moving forward ever since.

"I've made up my mind, Jay," I said. "I'm going."

He looked at me with a blank expression and sighed. "It's your decision."

I went off to Hawaii to start my senior season.

◆◆◆

Hawaii was no vacation. Practice began the moment we arrived and the coaches weren't easy on us. I didn't mind. I figured we needed the work. It was blazing hot and we needed to acclimate ourselves to the humidity. The game was going to be held at Aloha Stadium and televised in the States as the main event of a quadruple-header. Four California teams against four Hawaiian teams. I needed an excellent showing.

On the day of the game, our team was pumped up. John roamed the locker room shouting, banging guys on the shoulder pads and revving them up for the challenge at hand. I was off in my corner with my music. BeBe and CeCe Winans were caressing my nerves.

We were all trying to take care of those last minute details before we became a team entering into battle together for an entire season. I had grown to love these guys. We were a team with heart and character.

Most of the guys would be playing both ways this year, on offense and defense. That's the price you paid for attending a small private school with an enrollment of only four hundred and fifty students. Every player had to give more, every game. Working together, with one single goal, we were willing, even happy to play on both sides of the ball.

To people on the outside, however, we were simply the best team money could buy.

We got into our locker room huddle, bouncing up and down, shouting, and pumping our adrenaline up to light speed. Leading the pre-game chant, was none other than John "Wildman" Pearlman, who yelled out at the top of his lungs, "WHAT TIME IS IT?!" We responded with a roar, "GAME TIME!... GAME TIME!.. GAME TIME!" The sound bounced off the locker room walls, resounding in our ears, making us quiver with excitement.

The battle was about to begin. We turned to our coaches; ready to be led onto the field. There was nothing to do, but to do it.

The coaches, once smiling, grew extremely serious. They raised their arms in unison, directing us to settle down and take our seats. None of us knew what was going on, but we knew that it couldn't be good. The last thing we wanted to do was sit.

Coach Santini stepped before us with a somber expression.

"Boys, we got some bad news from the CIF Southern Section office. I'm not going to dance around with this thing. I'll give it to you straight." He cleared his throat and looked intently at each of us.

"As you know, we have a few players on our team in their fifth year of eligibility. And you know we've always gotten it approved. We've always come through for you." He paused and looked down at the floor.

He looked up, with distress written all over him. "Well, we did our best boys, but, they've denied our petitions on three of our players. I hate like hell to tell you this, but these three players won't be able to suit up tonight.

"Carl Sanderson, Bruce Stalker...Preston Sparks. I'm sorry guys."

We were in shock. Nobody knew what to do. The whole team just sat there, stunned. Santini broke the silence, trying to rally us.

"I say we get out there with what we have left, and show those bastards what this Valley Prep ball club is made of! Now, LET'S GO!"

Nobody moved an inch. We couldn't. We wouldn't. The coaches had let us down.

Preston stood up. "You said you would take care of it," he shouted.

"We tried, Preston," said Santini. "We really tried."

Coach Hutchinson fumbled. Santini looked at the floor. Neither of them could look us in the eye.

"You said you would take care of it!" Preston repeated, his voice quivering with rage. "You told me to trust you! I never wanted to be held back in the first place. That was what you wanted. I could have been at UCLA! Now

I'm ineligible. What am I supposed to do now?"

Neither coach answered. There was nothing they could say to the truth.

John Pearlman was the next player to stand up. What he had to say was to the point. "This is a bunch of bull."

John was right. We all knew it. None of us believed for a second that the coaches had gotten this news minutes before the game. There was no telling how long they had known.

They didn't want to tell us. They knew that the Hawaii trip would never have materialized if they had made this announcement before we left California. They had screwed up big time and they waited until we were ready to take the field to own up to it.

The worst part was that Preston was right. He could have been at UCLA. The coaches knew it, but they had done what was best for them, without a thought to how their decisions might affect a young athlete with his whole career hanging in the balance.

They didn't care about Preston. If they did, they would have bent over backwards to get him into UCLA. Instead they held him back, hoping to win the CIF championship, and then ride his coattails into the college ranks.

UCLA wasn't the only school. If the coaches had Preston listed as a senior the year prior, a hundred more recruiters would have been crawling all over the place trying to offer him a scholarship.

Now Preston's eyes were bloodshot and swollen. It was the first time I had seen him like this. He always held everything inside. But now, in the locker room, minutes before a game, it was all coming out. He sobbed so hard that it was difficult to take.

Almost every player in the room was crying as well. The coaches just stood there, hands on their hips or in their pockets, staring at the floor.

This was a sad moment. More than a few players got up and went over to Preston, putting a hand on his shoulder, his neck, anything to offer some comfort. I just sat there, tears streaming down my face. I burned holes through the coaches, but they wouldn't look at me.

Preston and I stared at each other for a while, and we both knew what it meant. It was all over. We were out of there.

Preston was the first to break the tense silence. "Derek, I think you should play."

I sat and thought for a long time. My teammates were thinking too. I was numb inside. Finally, I stood up and walked over to Preston.

"Take off your jersey," I said quietly. Privately.

He didn't question it. He just did it. I took off my No. 35 jersey and replaced it with his. I would be No. 5 for the rest of my career.

"I'll play for you," I said publicly.

The rest of the team followed, behind me, heading out into the tunnel to take the field. There was a complete absence of the usual electricity or sound. Every movement was calm and measured. Just cleats, smacking against the cement, on their way to the field.

The echo filled our heads as we marched in unison. Plastic thuds clacking against the ground to remind us that we were still a team. For the last time, we were still a team.

When we finally took the field, the first thing we thought was that we had walked onto the set of a science fiction movie.

Fog everywhere. There was an eerie quality throughout the entire stadium. Only it wasn't fog; it was steam. When the temperature reached 110 degrees on the field, they wet it down to cool it off. The result was a mountain of steam shooting off the Astro turf.

I've been in some hot places, after all, I'm from Texas, but this felt like we had landed on the Sun.

The team felt emotionally drained from the locker room drama, and it didn't take but a couple minutes of stretching to completely sap our energy.

This was a first for me; feeling exhausted before a game!

◆◆◆

The game? Let's not call it a game. Let's call it a joke. We were a joke. If I thought Cascade had humiliated us in the semis last season, I needed to think again. This game against Hawaii Prep had to rank as the most embarrassing experience I've ever had on a football field.

On paper it didn't look nearly as bad as it actually was. We lost 28-7, and I rushed for 63 yards on 16 carries. No, rushed isn't the right word. We didn't rush anywhere that day. We pushed, nudged and inched a few pitiful gains. It was awful.

We had just lost a starting defensive and offensive player in Bruce Stalker, and our starting wide receiver and free safety in Preston. There were no options for players; there was no relief.

The same eleven players were forced to play the entire game on a field in 110 degree heat.

We never got it going. We just watched the other team run by, without the power to even lift our arms.

On one play, Leon Lett, playing both ways for the first time, was in at tackle. He went down. After everyone had returned to the huddle, Leon was still on his stomach. A couple of us ran over to him. I knelt down near his head.

"Leon," I said into his ear, "are you hurt?"

"No," his answer came back in short breathy gasps.

"Are you sure that you're not hurt?" I repeated.

"Nuh....no."

"Well get up!" I panicked.

He rolled his eyes in my direction. "Can't."

And it was true. He couldn't. He was completely fatigued and dehydrated. It sounds funny now; but it was torturous then. This guy didn't even have the strength to stand up. We had to call time-out and carry him off the field.

The slaughter only grew worse from there.

Ugliest of all was what happened to Ray Jackson. In the second half of the game, he severely tore a ligament in his ankle. It was a nauseating sight. He would miss the entire season, and with it, any chance to play college football. In a split second, on one play, his dream was over. I had a feeling that the rest of our dreams were not very far behind.

33. COLLAPSE

Falling apart at the seams, the entire team sat slumped in their seats, deflated, silent, and in anguishing pain.

The score was 28-7. What a disaster.

For the first time in memory I wasn't the first one to choose a seat for the flight back home. I waited until the coaches found theirs and then sat as far away as possible. Preston sat with me. Neither of us wanted to get into a confrontation. We just wanted to go home.

All I could do was sit there and look out of the window. Stare and think. How is this going to all work out?

I knew that I'd be hearing from Uncle Jay, and that he'd be angry, but what would I say? What *could* I say to him?

I felt my heart pounding. If I left Valley Prep, where would I land? On a team with another Marcus Wright-Fair? On a team with a strong passing game? Or maybe on a team that didn't want to be caught within ten feet of a kid whose middle name was "Controversy."

The coaches were smart to wait until the last minute to break the bad news. They knew it would be difficult for me to transfer with the season already underway. Where could I go? Where would I live? How would I catch on with a new team in such a short time? I put my head in my hands while these thoughts spun around inside me. I kept going over them, again and again.

What did I do wrong? I had done what I was told to do and I did my part. I had worked hard, more than most people could ever imagine. I never asked questions or made trouble. The team and the game always came first. Still, here I was, standing on the edge, looking at the end of the line.

The only thing that kept me from going out of my mind was looking over at Preston. He was deep in thought too. I suspected what he must be thinking.

Preston was the one person in all of this who had received a really raw deal. He had been overlooked and dumped on since he arrived in California. Now here it was, all over again.

Preston, knowing that something big was about to happen, but he remained totally calm.

After he gave me his jersey in the Aloha Stadium locker room, he went straight to a pay phone and called Jay. When Jay answered, Preston couldn't keep it together. He had lost all of his usual quiet composure and it broke Jay's heart. When Tom heard what happened, well you can guess his response.

As I looked at Preston, I realized that he wasn't going crazy about what had transpired back in Hawaii. He was leaning back, relaxed, thumping the armrest to the beat of something he was listening to on his headset.

That was Preston. His way of dealing with a crisis was to watch the situation unfold, telling himself that he would deal with it as it came. I tried to do the same.

I stared out the window and let the thoughts turn in my mind for the rest of the flight. I put on my headset. BeBe and CeCe came to my aid with comfort and reassurance that this storm would pass. I sang along silently, *"Ain't no need to worry...what the night is going to bring...it'll be all over in the morning."*

Reality touched down with the plane at LAX. My question about when I would see Jay got answered right away.

I saw Jay and Tom coming toward us, walking fast. I was trying to think of something to say, but their expressions suggested that I keep quiet. They meant business and were ready to roll over anyone who stood in the way.

They grabbed Preston and me by the arms, without a word, and led us away from the group. Valley Prep was over.

Right then, Coach Hutchinson almost made the mistake of his life. He stepped forward to talk to Tom, maybe to try and explain. He felt close to Tom. Tom was the linebacker coach under Coach Hutchinson, who was the defensive coordinator. Even though Tom had supported Jay's campaign against Valley Prep by not returning as an assistant coach, Hutchinson felt he could reason with Tom. He was wrong. Tom was on a family mission.

Tom froze when he heard Coach Hutchinson's voice, turning slowly to face him. If looks could kill, Tom's face would have sent Hutchinson to meet his maker. If that look didn't finish the job, Tom's body language made it clear that he was packing something under his coat. When he spoke, it was barely more than a whisper.

"I got nothin' to say to you, sucker."

The deadly cold in his voice froze Hutchinson where he stood. The color drained from his face. Nobody moved as Tom turned back to Jay, waiting for a sign.

Jay, thinking...fingers twitching...finally shook his head...*No!* Preston and I kept walking.

Not another word was said. We left the team and the coaches standing there, looking as helpless as they must have felt. Tom walked away from them backwards, hand still in his coat pocket, shaking his head. Finally, he turned around and caught up.

And just like that, we were gone.

34. RUN

There wasn't much to say in the van. Preston and I, sitting behind the two fuming men, looked first at each other, then out of the window. We were both dumbfounded.

I tried to survey Jay's face in the rear-view mirror. He glared back at me stoned-faced for a second, but said nothing. He just looked straight ahead and drove.

No explosions, no shouting, just the hum of the engine.

Jay finally broke the silence. "I told you so," he said, hissing the words between his clenched teeth.

It was the only thing said for a long time. The atmosphere was tense. I let his statement sink in.

He was right; he had told us. I thought about it and realized that most of Jay's predictions about Valley Prep had come true.

The coaches didn't give a damn about Preston. They didn't give a damn about any of the other players, or me, for that matter. I saw it all as clearly as the smooth road ahead. But now that road was behind me.

I wondered how much of this unbelievable situation I'd brought on myself and how much had been dumped on me. Throughout the ride I began feeling like everything bad—the SAT results, the phony arrest report, the barrage of bad press, and now this, my cousin's ineligibility — had happened because I hadn't listened to Jay.

He drove straight to the Pearlman's house in Grant Hills.

Susie opened the door with her usual cheerful smile. "Welcome ho..."

Jay pushed me inside, glowering at Susie Pearlman. "Get your things," he said, his arms crossed in drill sergeant fashion. "I'll wait here."

I did what I was told.

Leaving the Pearlman's home was hard. As I shuttled arm loads of clothes, shoes, trophies and books from my room to Jay's van, where Preston waited in silence, I couldn't look straight at either Ron or Susie.

The Pearlmans just stood on their front lawn overwhelmed and confused. Susie cried. Ron paced nervously. Finally, Ron tried to step in and sort things out.

"Look here, Mr. Sparks," he stuttered.

Tom, standing along side of Jay, grabbed him and snarled, "Say something else, boy, and you're a dead man."

Ron saw that he was dealing with a crazy man who meant business. Maybe two crazy men! It was easy to see that Tom meant business. I felt badly because he didn't deserve the treatment he was getting from Jay or Tom, but I wasn't in the position to say anything.

I gathered up the rest of my things: my scrapbook, bulging with newspaper clippings, and a box of recruiting letters from various colleges.

I felt guilty, just taking everything and walking away. I stopped at the door on my way out and tried to smile. I never really saw if they smiled back. Jay fired up the van and we sped away.

◆◆◆

From the moment I first picked up a football, someone was there to teach me how to be a team player. That's always the first lesson any kid with gridiron dreams learns; put the team and the team's interests ahead of your own.

Cover your teammate's back, right or wrong, and cling to them like family. I felt this way about my Valley Prep teammates. How could I not? We were small in number and big on heart.

Put aside all of the other garbage for a moment, and we were just a bunch of kids who loved the game and wanted to make it our life. We were united in a common purpose and had become just like a family. It made me ache to leave them.

Those guys were my team. Now I was walking away without so much as an explanation. Losing contact with John was going to be the most difficult thing. He had become one of my best friends, a brother. I never even had a chance to say good-bye.

I needed help. I needed to know the right thing to do. On my own, I was helpless. The nightmare I was living was damning evidence of my own inadequacy. I sat alone for a long time, rubbing my eyes red.

A couple of hours passed with me crouched in a chair, praying. Slowly my mind began to settle, and as it did, I found direction.

I was tired of being wrong.

I grabbed the telephone and called my friend. John answered. I could tell from his voice that he was hesitant to accept my call.

John was angry. He was angry at the coaches, knowing that they could have done more to keep Preston and the other players eligible. They had done it for him without a problem.

He was angry at both Jay and Tom. He didn't like the way they had treated his parents when we left their house. I felt bad; I couldn't blame him. The only thing the Pearlmans had ever done was care.

I told John how much I sincerely appreciated all he and his family had done for me. I had never really thanked them before. Friends sometimes don't have to say those things, but mostly they just pass up their chances. I tried to express myself. The phone was fighting me.

We both fell silent. Neither one of us knew what was going to happen with Valley Prep, our futures, even our friendship; but we both knew what we wanted. We were going to get back on the field and fight tooth and nail to stay there. We left it at that. He felt confused and a little scared, but he didn't want to make me feel any worse.

"You take care, D."

I tried to speak. There was a long pause, and then the line went dead.

I had to say something to the team. I called Coach Hutchinson. He sounded defensive. He had all kinds of questions. I didn't have any answers. I didn't want to play into the blame game.

"I just wanted to make contact because I do care," I said. I apologized for the way events unfolded and expressed how much I wished that I could be out there on the field for the season opener.

"I don't know what's going to happen, Coach," I said, "but please tell the guys I'm going to miss them."

Hutchinson wanted to find out more about what Jay was planning for

Preston and me. I didn't want to talk about it. I hung up as quickly as I could.

That night, at Jay's, I couldn't sleep at all. It was the same way I'd felt when I first arrived in California; nervous, missing Mom, my relatives, Preston, and Omar. The only difference was, back then, I felt that I knew where I belonged and where I was heading.

I tossed and turned, and couldn't shake the feeling that I was out of place. I wanted to sneak out and go find my team.

What I did do, in the early morning hours, was write a letter to my teammates. I knew they were going to be hearing a lot of things from the coaches. I wanted them to hear the story from me, not Coach Hutchinson's or Santini's version of it.

I apologized for the way this had happened, explaining that it was all out of my control. I told them that I wished I could be playing with them this week...this season, but the situation was spun. I asked them to keep their heads up, play hard, and be proud of the team they had become. I missed them. I signed the letter, folded and sealed it and fell into a restless sleep.

I sent the letter to John, then called to tell him to expect it. He promised that he would read my letter in the locker room before the opening game.

◆◆◆

Events unfolded at light speed.

With school starting after we returned from Hawaii, it was clear that we weren't going to be attending Valley Prep. But where were we going? No one seemed to know and it made me uneasy.

The Valley Prep coaches were frantically trying to get Preston's eligibility cleared, with no luck. Besides, it was irrelevant. Preston and I knew Jay better than they did. He was through with them. Still, he wanted to keep Valley Prep in the dark about his plans. A transfer would be difficult enough without their meddling, so he played along.

To be safe, Jay released a statement to the media: Preston and I were returning to Texas at our mothers' request. I dreaded Jay's concocted story and it's eventual evolution. The first Los Angeles *Times* newspaper article was not merciful:

DEREK SPARKS PULLED FROM SCHOOL, MIGHT BE HEADED FOR TEXAS

The uncle of Derek Sparks, Southern California's top football prospect, removed the running back from Valley Prep...and said he will send him to Texas, where his high school career started three years ago.

Preston Sparks, a wide receiver and Derek's cousin, also has been pulled from Valley Prep and is headed to Texas, said Jay Sparks, their uncle. The move comes with the acquiescence of Valley Prep Coach J.K. Santini and ends a stormy relationship between the private school and Jay Sparks.

The move was triggered when Santini informed Preston Sparks just minutes before Valley Prep's season opening game in Hawaii that the CIF Southern Section had denied Sparks' request for a fifth year of eligibility. Two other Valley Prep players were denied eligibility and banned from the game against Hawaii Prep. In Valley Prep's 28-7 loss, Derek rushed for 63 yards in 16 carries.

Jay blamed Valley Prep for the eligibility ruling and pulled his nephews from the school. Preston had appealed the Southern Section's ruling and had been granted a hearing, a date he now will break.

Jay met the two players at the airport when they returned from Hawaii and brought them to his house in Inglewood. Neither player attended school this week.

Jay indicated earlier that Derek would stay in California and transfer to Mater Dei, a parochial school in Orange County.

Mater Dei's Coach Rollinson confirmed that the school had been contacted by Jay and said he would accept Derek to his team, provided the transfer had met CIF Southern Section eligibility rules.

But Jay changed plans after Derek's mother, June, arrived from Texas and insisted the boys return with her.

Derek, 17, was unavailable for comment...but stated all summer that he wished to continue at Valley Prep despite ill feelings between his uncle and the school. Derek, a 6-foot, 210-pound senior, was selected the Sophomore State Player of the Year by Cal-Hi Sports Magazine at Central High School after moving from Wharton Texas. He enrolled at Valley Prep in the spring and was named the Times' Running Back of the Year after he rushed for 1,944 yards and 35 touchdowns.

When asked whether Derek wanted to leave Valley Prep, Jay said, "Whatever we say, he's going to do."

> *Santini encouraged the move despite his fondness for the players and the damage to his team the loss represents.*
>
> *"I'm sorry to see them go and I'm sorry to see the boys go through this, but I told Jay that if this is causing that many family problems, they should go to another school."*

Reading the article triggered my mind into trying to distinguish the hype from the truth. It was a tough assignment.

The papers claimed that my mom was demanding our return to Texas. There was some truth to this. She went into shock after a phone conversation with Jay in which he told her that he was pulling me out of school. She slammed the receiver and immediately boarded a plane to Los Angeles.

I shared her confusion. The news report was the first I had heard of my confirmed transfer to Mater Dei. I had never even heard of the school, and I didn't know what a parochial school was, but it sure didn't sound like a place to run the football.

I thought that things couldn't get worse, but I was wrong. The worst was yet to come. The next day's *Daily News* Sports headline hit me like a ton of bricks.

SPARKS PAIR WON'T PLAY FOR SUNDEVILS: DISPUTE PROMPTS VALLEY PREP COACH TO ASK COUSINS TO PURSUE TRANSFERS

Running back Derek Sparks and his cousin, wide receiver Preston Sparks, were kicked off the Valley Prep High School football team...by Coach J.K. Santini because of a dispute with their uncle and legal guardian, Jay Sparks, Santini said...

Kicked off! I couldn't believe what I was reading. I was stunned. Didn't they know what that kind of bad publicity could do to me? Saying that I was kicked off the team made it look like I was a troublemaker.

College recruiters would read it, they'd read between the lines, then they'd move on to the next prospect. No one would make an effort to get the real story.

The coaches understood what would hurt me, what would ruin my chances. They were going for the jugular. They wouldn't relent; not as long as they could funnel media scrutiny away from themselves and their program.

> *Derek was considered to be the top high school running back in the country after running for 1,944 yards and 35 touchdowns last season.*
>
> *Preston played quarterback last season and was supposed to switch to wide receiver this year, but was declared ineligible by the CIF Southern Section shortly before the Sundevils' season opener against Hawaii Prep in Hawaii...because he is in his fifth year of high school.*
>
> *The CIF Southern Section is scheduled to hear his appeal Wednesday, but that probably won't be necessary.*
>
> *Jay Sparks said each player's mother wants them to move back to Texas with them. Derek and Preston are from Texas, but moved to California with Jay two years ago to better their chances of getting a college scholarship.*
>
> *Coach Santini said that Derek and Preston had done nothing wrong but that their uncle had become a disruptive influence.*
>
> *"An unfortunate situation developed," Santini said, "and we have 28 other players to worry about."*

I dropped the newspaper to the floor. It was the first time I had ever seen a newspaper refer to me in the past tense. "Derek *was* considered to be the top high school running back in the country..." I felt like a teenager who had just read his own obituary.

So that was it. I knew the press would only get worse from there. I felt sick to my stomach. From the first day they gave me the guided tour around campus, I knew that my coaches were shady, but I always believed they liked me and wished for my success in life.

That's when the phone rang.

I stood there with one unpacked suitcase; clothes, newspaper articles, and college letters strewn across the bed. Something inside was telling me not to pick it up.

"Hello," I said tentatively.

The voice on the other end was choked with fury. "You traitor, who the hell do you think you are?"

I couldn't make out who it was. I knew it had to be a coach or administrator from Valley Prep.

Heavy breathing...then the voice continued before I could get in a word. "After all we did for you, you ungrateful piece of crap! This is how you show your appreciation? Walking out without so much as a word.

"I'll tell you what, you bastard," the voice spat into the telephone receiver, "you'll never play organized football again. We're gonna see to that.

"You can kiss your senior year good-bye, and you can take all of those letters you got from colleges and shove them up your butt. That's all the good they're gonna do you!"

The voice became quiet, almost calm. "We made an investment in you, gave you the best of everything, and you had no problem with any of it. And now you think you can just spit in our faces and walk away? This is your wake up call, kid."

Jay and the coaches had waged war on each other and the bullets were spinning in circles around me. Now, with this phone call, I was feeling them deep down in my gut. My clothes and my life lay before me in a messy heap.

People move in circles when a point is hard to reach. I was at the point where I didn't even know myself anymore. I was just a 17-year old high school football player who had already taken cash, accepted gifts and lived in houses provided by two different schools in as many years. Why? Because some greedy, demented, selfish, fame-seeking and corrupt family members, coaches and administrators had given me the green light.

With my fists clenched hard, my mind stewed over the past two years. I realized with a jolt that I wasn't looking up at the machine; I was in it. Grease, plastic and dollar signs.

This was my wake-up call.

35. RESOLVE

I don't know if all men remember the exact moment they made the transition from boy to man. I hear a lot of guys talking about their first serious relationship with a woman. Others say it has to do with shared feelings between them and their fathers. Or their first child being born. Regardless, most people say there is a moment when a boy leaves childhood behind and accepts his role in the world as a man.

This was my moment.

I cried for a long time. Cried like I never had before, loud and hard. I cried for the things I had lost, the things I had given up, and the things I was afraid I'd never have. I cried because I was afraid. Afraid of losing my dream and afraid of the person I had become.

My father stood next to me in the shadows, shaking his head and laughing as though hearing a familiar joke. He slapped me on the back, shut the door, and stepped back into Wharton, Texas.

But Texas was far away from me, and imagining my father's reaction made me wake up and see how pitiful I looked. This big ol' boy crying like a baby.

I had a decision to make. I could walk away from the conflict and keep crying, or I could step up, and take the matter into my own hands like a man. Like a man!

It was an easy choice. I had no reason to feel sorry for myself. I had all the God-given talent in the world and it damn sure didn't look to me like my career was over.

I started to laugh at how ridiculous I looked and how pathetic I'd become. I laughed at all of the grown-up people I had dealt with who spent all of their maturity manipulating kids. It was so ridiculous that I had to laugh.

In my mind, it was resolved. I was going to show them all. I was a man. A good man. I was going to play the game I loved honestly and fairly, and I was going to win.

◆◆◆

My mind was made up; it was time to move. Fast! I had decisions to make. I needed to get on a team somewhere and I needed to kick some butt.

The media were trying to write me off. The only way I could answer was to do my talking where I had always done it best; on the football field.

My mother's arrival from Texas was a huge help and did a lot to clear my confusion. She hugged me like when I was a kid and told me everything was going to be okay. Her comfort was a confirmation that it would be.

I cornered Jay the minute he walked in from work, pumping him for information about Mater Dei. Instead of letting things get taken care of, this time I took control of the questions. I asked why he had chosen a Catholic school in Orange County, some fifty miles away.

I sat Moms and Jay down and expressed how much I loved them and appreciated their guidance. I told Jay how sorry I was that I hadn't listened to him in the past. I took responsibility for all the things that had gone wrong.

"It's time to move forward," I said as diplomatically as I knew how. "I'm not going to let this chain of events derail me from my dream of earning a scholarship to a major university and I'm not going to stop until I do."

Both Moms and Jay looked at my new confidence with amazement. I'm not sure they liked it, but they saw that I was serious.

"Now tell me more about what you really have in mind," I said directly to Jay, meeting him eye to eye.

Then he told me about Robert Epps. He called him Bob.

Robert Epps was an old friend of Jay's. He was an older white man who had made himself a ton of money. A man with his fingers in a lot of pies—real estate, stocks, investments—he was always on the make for another profitable deal. He was one of the potential investors Jay had been pitching with his Texas Connection.

I learned that a part of the tension between Jay and the Valley Prep coaches stemmed from Jay throwing Bob Epps's name into their discussions. Jay told them that if they couldn't, or wouldn't honor their promises, he knew someone with enough clout and means to make things happen. He didn't need Valley Prep. He could take his boys and make it happen somewhere else.

But Robert Epps was not an easy sell. Jay told him the latest scandal involving Valley Prep, Preston and me. Epps was sympathetic, but not terribly eager to become involved. Especially if his involvement meant going into his pocket.

It took a lot of convincing, but finally Robert Epps proposed an idea that sounded palatable to Jay. Epps had a piece of property, a house, just a few blocks from Mater Dei High School in Orange County. The house was currently vacant. He proposed that Jay enroll us in Mater Dei and move us into the house.

Jay liked the idea right away, but there were a lot of details that needed to be ironed out. Since demanding that the Pearlmans surrender custody of me, he had to reestaablish himself as my legal guardian. But he couldn't just pick up his business and move to Orange County.

The school posed another obstacle. They could only enroll us if we had established legal residency in their district.

Even as he was speaking, posing his questions, I saw the plan. I smiled as he spoke. I respected how fast his mind worked.

Now it was clear why my mother was here, and it was not to take us back to Texas. The only way around the guardianship and residency issues would be for me and my mother to live together in Orange County.

Jay arranged a job for Mom while she lived in California. Things being what they were in Wharton, a decent paying job was plenty of incentive for her to stay for a while. Not to mention that a good sized house to live in was a nice change from the projects back home in Texas.

Now it was time to talk about Mater Dei High School. By now, I didn't care what kind of school it was. I just had to know if it was a place I could start at tailback, gain a lot of yards and attract college recruiters.

Jay's response was mixed.

Mater Dei had a reputation around the country as a powerhouse basketball school. The football program was less decorated at that time, but it wasn't far behind.

Led by Coach Rollinson, whom I rated as one of the greatest high school football coaches in California history, the Mater Dei Monarchs had made it to the first round of the CIF Southern Section playoffs within his two years as head coach.

The team was gaining momentum and I got excited about the possibility of being coached by a legend. They'd had an impressive tailback, Kealy Cifford, who graduated and signed his letter of intent to Oregon University. Now the position was wide open.

Last years quarterback, Danny O'Neil, had graduated and gone to Oregon too. I felt better knowing that Pac-10 recruiters were hanging around the campus.

I wanted to know how many high caliber players remained at Mater Dei. Quarterbacks, in particular. Being on a team without a passing threat only allows opposing teams to key on the running game. That spelled hell for me and would make it nearly impossible to gain the kind of yardage I needed in my senior year.

I also had concerns about Preston. Would he regain his eligibility? If so, would he be forced into another predicament similar to the one at Valley Prep. He needed a ton of receptions at the receiver position to rejuvenate the interest of schools like UCLA.

The answer to the quarterback question came in the form of a kid named Billy Blanton. Billy was a junior who had led the freshman and sophomore teams to undefeated seasons. He had the starting position sown up and he had all the tools necessary to get the job done. Heck, what can I say about Billy Blanton? Even his name sounded like the name of a great quarterback.

The other issue I had to deal with was Mater Dei being a Catholic school. I've always considered myself pretty religious, but I wasn't Catholic. I didn't know Catholic traditions or beliefs. Jay assured me that there were other non-Catholics attending the school, so I relaxed about that concern.

I wanted to speak to the family before things really got rolling and I was in too deep. I made sure Preston was in on the discussion. I waited for the small talk to end. I wanted everyone's full attention. Clearly, in my mind, I was fighting for my dream, my future, my life.

I looked at them all and told them that I appreciated Robert Epps coming to our rescue. I explained that the new arrangement would have to be above board and legal for me to go along with it.

"We'll have to pay rent for the house," I said, looking straight at Jay. "Nothing under the table.

"If we don't have the money, I'm willing to work." I needed my mother and Jay to be in complete agreement. They were.

I was grateful that my mom would have a job; but to my way of thinking, it needed to be a real job. Mom liked the maturity she saw in me, but drew the line at being told how to conduct herself.

"You just worry about getting your butt to class and I'll worry about me," she said smiling.

They may have interrupted me while I spelled out my requirements, but my message was clear.

All that remained was for all of us to pay a visit to the school and to move into Robert Epps's house to establish Orange County residency.

The day we visited the Mater Dei campus it was surprising how much I actually liked the school. It was bigger than Central and had excellent facilities.

Mater Dei was a private school like Valley Prep. They used the football stadium at school as a practice facility. They played their home games at Orange Coast College; in a huge stadium nearby nicknamed "The Pit," because it was constructed a couple of feet into the ground.

Orange County was conservative, predominantly white. It was a nice place to live and the house was nearly as spacious as the one we'd enjoyed while at Valley Prep. But I would have played on the moon at that point in my career.

We started classes the next day, and worked out with the team that afternoon.

Preston and I received a warm reception from the team. I recalled my first day at Central. There was a big difference. These guys had all heard of Preston and me and were glad to welcome us on board. They wanted a winning team and thought we could help them get there.

Above all, from my standpoint, there was no Marcus Wright-Fair to be pushed aside with my arrival.

The coaches were different too; they had character. Although they were as happy as could be, they remained cautious, waiting to find out if my eligibility was official. None of us knew for sure how that would play out. But one thing was certain, it would be by the rules.

Last month, Derek Sparks was getting ready for Valley Prep's season; now he's at Mater Dei.

Sparks might play for Mater Dei this year

◆◆◆

Jay took us to the CIF Southern Section Commissioner's office to petition Preston's eligibility and to discuss our transfer. The commissioner, Stan Thomas, seemed like an understanding guy. He had a judge's demeanor but in his eyes I noticed a kindly twinkle, like a much-loved spiritual leader.

Of course he was aware of the controversy that had been brewing. He said that he wanted to see us get our education and perform well on the field. But his first priority was to sort through everything in order to insure that rules hadn't been violated.

He scheduled a hearing in two days in which he'd review our transcripts and rule on our transfers.

I don't think that Preston or I said much of anything at that meeting. It's hard to speak with a lump in your throat. We thanked him and left.

We were all depending on the commissioner to sort through our statements, the transcripts and facts, and render a fair decision. We knew, though, that he was going to dig.

How many of our dealings at Valley Prep would come back to haunt us? How would the Valley Prep administration respond to our charges? What would happen if the media got a hold of our meeting?

We did everything we could to keep the news quiet, but I knew that it was just a matter of time before the lid blew off the scandal. Waiting for answers wasn't going to be easy.

◆◆◆

That night I received a phone call from Coach Hutchinson.

"How are you doing?" he asked.

"Fine," I lied. "Just fine. And how's the team doing?"

"We're playing extremely well." He lied too.

I had read the newspapers and we both knew that they weren't playing well at all.

The week before, they'd lost to Santa Monica, 20-9. They were upset by Western the week before that. Even worse, my good friend John Pearlman, was in terrible shape.

Now in his senior (fifth) year, John chipped a bone in his shoulder, an injury so painful that it forced him to lie on the field for a half minute or so after each play, writhing in agony. But Johnny always got up and continued to play. It's what he was taught and what the machine required.

When John went to the coaches and asked to see a real doctor, they said that he needed to learn the difference between being injured and being hurt. He didn't need a doctor. So John sucked it up, fought through the pain, and continued to play.

The coaches did arrange for John to have a standing appointment every week with a "Magic Man" who did his doctoring behind a white curtain, injecting John with enough cortisone to numb his painful shoulder.

After a few hits, even the injections couldn't mask his pain. So John would bite down hard and continue playing.

Eventually, the chipped bone had formed a jagged edge next to the tendon. Every time John made a bone-crushing hit on his opponent, the bone hacked away at the tendon like a dull knife. With every tackle, the impact weakened his shoulder a little more. Soon it reached the point where he couldn't use his arm.

Did the coaches hustle him off the field to see a real doctor or a specialist?

No. At half-time they had him injected with more cortisone and sent him back out, onto the field, with one arm working.

John, the stalwart, was getting his chance to prove to the world how tough he was, not knowing that he was throwing away any future chances he had of playing football. Ever!

John finally felt compelled to see a doctor after the chipped bone cut the last thread of the tendon, severing it completely. He couldn't lift his arm. Still, the coaches showed little emotion. *Pearlman's done, time to recruit another young stud.*

The health of the players was the last thing Coach Hutchinson or Santini were thinking about.

◆◆◆

As Hutchinson's small talk ended, he got to the point.

"You know, Derek," he said, "it's too bad that you slammed the door on some pretty big deals we were working on here for you."

Yeah, right. Deals he was hooking up for all of us. Deals that he would benefit from.

"Some of my friends have already contacted me about your abilities, Derek. And of course they want to know about this hearing thing." Hutchinson paused, waiting for me to respond.

He knew about the hearing. What else did he know? Where was this going? I didn't say anything for fear that our conversation was being recorded. I didn't put anything past Hutchinson.

He sighed. "What are you going to tell them, Derek? I'm afraid that it's all up to you, Sparks. ...And what you boys are going to say at that hearing day after tomorrow.

There it was. He knew about the hearing. I was in deep. The phone rattled in my hand.

He asked me if I understood. I told him that I would seriously think about what he had said.

"You do that," he said quietly. "I'd love to see you go on to play some more football somewhere." He hung up.

I sat there for a minute to absorb the conversation. Then I let it go. I wasn't going to allow myself to become distracted by this cloak and dagger stuff. If Valley Prep was going to ruin me, so be it. It wouldn't happen without the best fight I could put up, and the first step was to get back on the football field.

I decided to let Jay and my mom worry about my dilemma. I wanted to keep my mind on football. I tried to dismiss any thoughts of being banned from the game or losing my eligibility. I would take it one step at a time, making sure that I was ready to play if the chance came. Jay would handle the rest.

Jay sat me down the night before the hearing. He looked at me intently. We had been through a lot over the past two years, and I had gotten used to the clipped tone and expressionless face he used when he dealt with me on serious issues.

This night was different, though. His tone was soft and his eyes were a little moist. "You know we may be headed for some hard times, Derek," he began softly.

"Yeah, I figured," I responded.

"A lot of things might be said that will hurt you. Are you ready for all of that?"

"I guess," I said.

"You gotta know, there's no turning back once we start."

"I just want to play football," I said. Could Jay hear the pleading, praying desperation in my voice?

"Yeah, well, there's no guarantee that that's gonna happen. We'll do the best we can, but God only knows what's ahead."

"Are you going to tell them about the deal at Valley Prep?"

Uncle Jay looked at me, no, through me, with a distant gaze as if he was in a trance.

"I don't know. I really don't."

He dropped his head, as if it were a heavy ball, going deep into thought, staring at the floor. He finally spoke again, but his eyes remained fixed downward.

"What do you think I should do?"

It took awhile, but I found the answer. "Forward or backwards."

He looked up at me slowly and I smiled at him, sending him a wave of reassurance.

We had no idea what would happen from here. Jay had made some poor choices, but I understood his intentions. He was my uncle, my childhood hero, and the closest thing to a father I'd ever known. He felt sure that I would accept that he had done his best. He smiled back.

36. The Trial

Jay sang like a bird that morning in the CIF Southern Section office. He sang like Aretha Franklin. He told it all, most without any prompting from Commissioner Thomas.

It was amazing to me that Valley Prep had sent only one representative, a man I'd never met who had just assumed a post as the vice principal at the school. Maybe Coach Hutchinson thought that I had heeded his warnings.

Evidently, the coaches at Valley Prep didn't think that our accusations held any threat to them. They had obviously underestimated Jay.

Before the commission, Jay recalled the day Coach Hutchinson called me in Texas, and how he later illegally recruited me from Central High. He also explained the deal to bring Preston out to California from Texas. Jay admitted that neither of us paid tuition at Valley Prep.

He told the commission that the coaches changed Preston's grades and made him a sophomore instead of a junior. It was done, he said, without Preston's consent. When Preston protested the coaches said, "Don't worry, we'll handle it. The founder-principal, Pop Wilson, has friends in the CIF Southern Section office who owe us favors. We do this all the time."

He spilled the illegalities of Tom's situation: How he was hired on as one of the highest paid assistant coaches in the state; and how they created other job titles for Tom, like general caretaker and boarding supervisor, in order to pay him more money.

Jay told it all! Mr. Thomas and the Executive Committee members listened in disbelief, shaking their heads throughout his testimony.

Mr. Thomas asked Preston and me if we held Jays statements to be true. Preston looked at me. We both hesitated for a moment. Then we both started speaking simultaneously.

Preston stood up first and spoke with passion. He did exactly as he was told when he came to California, he said. He was completely unaware that they had put him back a year. The coaching staff had reassured him daily that everything would work out. He recited the coaches favorite line. "We'll take care of it. Just run the football."

Preston talked about the classes he never attended and passing grades that he never earned.

Mr. Thomas turned the question to me. Had I received passing grades for any classes I didn't take?

I looked at Jay, unsure of what to say. He nodded his head in accordance.

I answered, "Yes."

Preston interjected. "Derek went to class. He's focused. I'm the one who messed up."

Mr. Thomas had a frown the size of the state of Texas. We were in a hole that kept collapsing. Deeper into the mud.

Tom stood up to speak. He followed Jay's lead and dropped his observations and his participation on the commission.

"When you take a young man out of class and drive him to your grandfather's bank during class hours, you are contributing to him not getting to class." He was talking about Coach Santini's role in our delinquency.

Tom continued, revealing how the coaches had first-hand knowledge of players using steroids. Kids with average physiques who enrolled at Valley Prep doubled their muscle mass, seemingly overnight. He named names.

Tom talked about the coaches inappropriate relationships with 16- and 17-year-old girl students at the school. He threw in some allegations about cocaine use. Preston and I didn't know about that part of the Valley Prep story, but it didn't surprise us that Tom did.

Tom was on a roll and he hadn't finished. He brought up a discussion that had taken place over pizza one night between Jay and him and the coaches. This was during the time that Marcus Wright-Fair's dad had come in to raise hell over his son's lack of carries. The coaches responded by suggesting Marcus transfer if he couldn't handle the situation.

The coaches, Tom alleged, were tired of dealing with Marcus Wright-Fair's father, and were not looking forward to a bad attitude from Marcus. They thought that it would just be easier to get rid of him. So, according to Tom, they sat at that pizza parlor and pieced together a plan. They were going to plant drugs on Marcus and tip-off the police to ensure his incrimination.

Two coaches plotting to frame a student! A student with probably the brightest future of any kid in California. All of this so they wouldn't have to deal with him sticking up for his rights.

Mr. Thomas and the executive members of the commission looked completely overwhelmed. There was more than one red face sitting at that table. One or two of the distinguished middle-aged men seemed stricken with rage.

Tom went on. He believed that the coaches would have followed through, but Jay had spoken up at the meeting. So long as he had anything to do with Valley Prep, Jay said, no kid was going to be framed, blackballed or harmed. The coaches had backed off for the moment.

Marcus was such an honorable guy and popular team player that, without anyone to conspire with, the plan never materialized. But, man, even I was shaking my head at this point.

Tom had more to say. He brought out details of how officials at Valley Prep bribed someone within the San Gabriel juvenile court system to get my custody switched from Jay to the Pearlmans. Making me a "601 Ward of the Court" ensured that I wouldn't be able to leave Valley Prep. It guaranteed that Jay couldn't pull me out of their school.

Tom revealed the coaches' connection at the Juvenile Corrections Department, a former football coach and student advisor at Valley Prep. Then he confirmed that it was Valley Prep's cash and power that pushed the case through the system.

Tom wasn't through. He hit Coach Hutchinson with the accusations that his college degrees were, in fact, illegitimate.

The room went crazy, and even Jay had to stand up and say, "Whoa, hold it, hold it! Lets not get into all of this personal stuff. Let's talk about our boys and whether we can get them back into school and back on the football field. All of this other stuff...well, this isn't the time."

It was too late; the damage was done.

While the commissioners took a short recess, we couldn't break from our thoughts of what could happen. Would we be thrown out of the district?

Would we be banned from football completely? Would the commission send us back to Texas? We sat and waited for the judgment. Sat and waited.

◆◆◆

Mr. Thomas didn't render a judgment that day. He said that he needed time to digest the testimony and to consult with the other members of the executive committee.

He noted, however, that it was his position that we were misled by the coaches at Valley Prep. Tentatively, he cited them with a "510 Violation," *"The use of undue influence by coaches and staff members to retain students as residents at their school."*

The "510 Violation" makes the student ineligible for any high school athletic program for an entire year. It holds the school in contempt as well, jeopardizing their standing with the CIF Southern Section.

Commissioner Thomas didn't excuse Preston and me from skipping classes. That was our responsibility as student-athletes. Our chances of meeting the requirements for academic eligibility were murky. And therefore, all of our hopes of playing football at Mater Dei hung in the balance.

I stood there feeling helpless. Mr. Thomas scanned the room before speaking. "I'll need to review the Sparks's transcripts. If their grades are authentic, without any violations, I will reinstate them immediately."

It took a minute to sink in.

We had won. They were allowing us to play for Mater Dei High School. I closed my eyes tight, savoring the sentence he had just uttered. My heart was one step closer to the field.

If he received the transcripts that day, I would be cleared to play in the game against Tustin on Friday. I was a ball of energy. I just needed someone to point me in the right direction.

It wasn't that simple. Commissioner Thomas and the executive committee announced that there would be a full scale investigation into our allegations against Valley Prep. We would all be subpoenaed. They were expecting us to appear and testify about the scandal we had just exposed.

Commissioner Thomas continued. "There have been some very strong accusations against Valley Prep. Today we heard one side of the story; we'd like to hear the other side, as it relates to a request for waiver of CIF S.S. Rule 202.

"If anyone else would like to make a declaration, we need to know. Would the Valley Prep staff like to make a statement?"

The man who had identified himself as the new vice principal stood up and addressed all of the issues in one flat statement.

"This is my first week as acting vice principal of Valley Prep. I had no previous affiliation with the school, but everybody I talked to has spoken very highly of both Derek and Preston. We certainly wish them all the success and happiness at Mater Dei High School, and we will be more than happy to respond to all allegations in written form."

There would be an encore. My feelings of victory were chilled right then and there. Valley Prep's reaction made me nervous. Whatever their response, it would be vicious and swift. They walked in shadows and waited for the opportunity to cast me face down in the mud. My reputation couldn't stand any more mud. But the machine was in full control. I'd have to wait and see what their move would be.

The next day's newspapers told me all I needed to know:

SPARKS' ALLEGATIONS GET VALLEY PREP INVESTIGATED
Improprieties cited at CIF Southern Section board hearing.

TESTIMONY PUTS VALLEY PREP IN A BAD LIGHT
Players' families accuse Valley school of grade tampering.

VALLEY PREP IS ACCUSED OF FAKING FOUR ATHLETES' LIVING ARRANGEMENTS
Using 5th year players, nothing new for Valley Prep.

VALLEY PREP CHARGED WITH USING 5TH-YEAR PLAYERS ALLEGATIONS PROMPT VALLEY PREP PROBE

An investigation into the Valley Prep High School athletic department was ordered by the CIF Southern Section Executive Committee...after the committee heard allegations of grade tampering, free tuition and recruiting violations, CIF Southern Section Commissioner Stan Thomas said.

The allegations were made by brothers Tom and Jay Sparks during a hearing on the eligibility of their nephews, Derek and Preston Sparks, who left Valley Prep last week and enrolled at Mater Dei Catholic High School in Santa Ana...

"I heard accusations I never heard before," Thomas said. "Probably the most shocking thing I have heard in my 20 years of association with athletics, you don't get this kind of stuff on the NCAA level."

Valley Prep head football coach J.K. Santini denied all accusations.

"The Sparks family has a disagreement with Valley Prep to start with," he

said. "We feel they're doing this to get back at Valley Prep."

Valley Prep officials are accused of changing Preston Sparks' grades last year to keep him eligible to play baseball, Thomas said.

If that proves to be true, Valley Prep may have to forfeit the WAC 1-A Division baseball championship it won last year.

Jay Sparks testified that Derek, who attended Valley Prep last season, and his cousin, Preston, were provided with room and board, and tuition free schooling during the 18 months they attended Valley Prep.

Santini said the Sparks' received financial aid, which is based on need, and were charged tuition for the costs not covered by financial aid.

"I do not know for a fact what the arrangement was, but I do know we had a collection problem with them," Coach Santini said. "The CIF Southern Section is fully aware of our financial aid program."

It was also charged that Valley Prep assistant football coach Hutchinson recruited Derek Sparks from his hometown of Wharton, Texas, to first play for Central in Long Beach when he was the head coach there, then for Valley Prep.

Coach Hutchinson said a friend of the Sparks family approached him first, but Hutchinson insisted that he did not actively recruit Derek.

"At Central, I could find a running back around the corner," he said. "I didn't have to go to Wharton, Texas..."

I thought it was strange that the Valley Prep officials had so much to say to the press, but hadn't defended the school at the hearing. I thought that maybe they knew something that we didn't.

They were going to deny everything and paint us as a bunch of hicks who refused to pay our bills. It was the opening volley and I knew the game would get uglier.

The late edition of the *Los Angeles Times* convinced me of it:

"It's buffoonery," Hutchinson said. "When it is examined point by point, there isn't a prayer (of proving the charges)..."

Hutchinson admitted that Preston was "deficient academically," but insisted the school had no reason to mislead him regarding eligibility.

"What do we gain by that?" he said. "Once this is out in the open, the witch hunt will reverse. Our books are open. Everything they have said will be discredited."

Hutchinson said he could not understand the CIF Southern Section's investigation.

> *"I don't know why they did it," he said. "Maybe they did it to get the Sparks out of their hair. The Sparks group is a wild bunch."*

It hurt to hear my coach say this. He went on to slam Jay the best he could.

> *Hutchinson insisted that Jay Sparks is manipulating Derek and the All-American tailback never wanted to leave Valley Prep.*
> *"I have a message on my voice mail," Coach Hutchinson said, referring to a tape recording made last week, when Sparks left the school. "He's sniffling. He said he didn't know what to do. He said, 'Coach, tell the guys I miss them.'*
> *"Jay is a school shopper. He's marketing this kid, and it's that simple. Derek is a pawn."*
> *"It's a given that he is going to be a pro, and that he'll bring some money into the Sparks family. If he ever makes enough to buy his mom a house, or his uncle a new carpet cleaning truck, he will do it because Derek is so giving. But that decision will be made for him. It's a real sad deal."*

Reading Hutchinson's comments told me that he did, indeed, tape our telephone conversations. I was on notice. I needed to keep my eyes open and my mouth shut at all times.

The next day's hearing found all of us, the Sparks family and Valley Prep, in the same room with the commission. It was a face-off between four Sparks men and a pep squad of Valley Prep coaches, administrators, lawyers, and friends of the program.

So much had been made of the hearing that even reporters were allowed to attend.

For five straight hours ugly accusations, shouting, cursing and threats were flying around us.

Valley Prep, standing on their record and their reputation, presented a mound of papers, but had little to say to counter any of our charges. Jay and Tom had already stated their case.

Nonetheless, in spite of their apparent lackluster performance at the hearing, Valley Prep bided time waiting to fire their next shot.

We were told that when Mr. Thomas received transcripts from Valley Prep, he would make the ruling on my eligibility. That was the only way I could play in Friday's game.

Valley Prep didn't miss a trick. After the commission called for the transcripts, there was a long delay before the school sent the documents. When the official documents finally reached the CIF office, it was discovered that they were invalid. The Valley Prep principal, Pop Wilson, had sent them unsigned.

I could just hear Pop Wilson, Santini, and Hutchinson cackling over their latest maneuver. They wanted to make me sweat.

Wednesday: No official transcripts, no clearance. I continued to practice with the team, waiting for word and the chance to compete.

Thursday: No signature. Valley Prep told the CIF that Pop Wilson was out of town. There was no way to reach him and he was the only one who could sign the documents.

Out of town?

Friday: The media picked up the story and immediately began fanning the flames. "Will Sparks play?" stories ran on page one in all the local newspapers.

WAITING ON WORD: IF SPARKS GETS OK TO PLAY, HIS PRESENCE WILL BE FELT

Derek Sparks would be a shot in the arm for the Mater Dei offense. It's up to the CIF Southern Section to OK his transfer.

No word from Pop Wilson. The people at the CIF Southern Section office became involved in trying to track him down. No one could detect where he was hiding, but I knew in my heart that he was somewhere in town.

◆◆◆

Friday night arrived and Valley Prep's time had run out. They had exhausted their list of excuses. I was going to play, I was just waiting for the word.

There must have been twenty thousand fans in that college stadium. I couldn't believe it. A football stadium, jammed full of fans, cheered so loudly the night was electric.

At Valley Prep we were lucky to draw a couple hundred people. Maybe a thousand on a good night. Now I was standing before tens of thousands of people, many of them there just to see if I would play. The pressure poured down on me.

I was dressed and ready to go, still waiting to receive the word. Down on the sidelines, a few NFL players from the Los Angeles Rams who played at the nearby Anaheim Stadium, came out to see what all the shouting was about. They wanted to see for themselves if I was all that. Was this Sparks kid worth all the commotion in the media?

The Mater Dei principal and CIF Southern Section office were working frantically to find Pop Wilson. Mater Dei's athletic director stood next to me on the sidelines with a cellular phone. When Commissioner Thomas held the transcripts in his hands, he would call in and deliver the go-ahead.

The crowd was fired up, chanting "WE WANT SPARKS! WE WANT SPARKS!" I hadn't played a single down and they knew who I was.

It came down to one cellular phone and one call. I knew that Commissioner Thomas and Mater Dei were doing everything they could to make this happen.

I kept looking to the athletic director, hoping I could make the phone ring by sheer willpower. Nothing.

The opening kickoff came and went. I was in agony. Still no word. All I could do was pace the sidelines and watch. Kevin Greene, the Rams star linebacker, came over from time to time to ask if there was any word. Nothing.

By half-time the phone remained quiet, and I was so tense I couldn't stand still. Mater Dei was not playing well. They were down 14-0, but the game was still in reach. If only I could get in.

We came out of the locker room after the half, with no change in status. I started the third quarter in the same spot I'd spent the first half.

Half way through the third quarter, the cellular phone rang. I nearly jumped out of my skin. It was Stan Thomas, the Commissioner. I began stretching my legs out and getting my mind focused. All I needed was the word and I'd be ready to take the field.

The athletic director called me over. Thomas had received the transcripts, but there was a problem. He needed a couple more days to sort it out.

"Problem!?" I shouted above the noisy din. "What problem?" But it didn't matter. I knew that the Valley Prep guys wouldn't lay down this easy. They swore that I'd never play another down of football and that was one promise they aimed to keep.

I felt crushed. This game was over, and I didn't know how many I'd miss. Valley Prep must have thrived on knowing that they could meet every challenge I could overcome with a more devious response than the time before.

The guys from the Rams were reassuring. They told me to cheer up; they'd return next week. But I couldn't hear a thing. My mind was a million miles away, trying to figure what the next move would be. It was a chess match. My future was the prize.

We lost the game.

37. CHECK

Valley Prep was playing their cards from a loaded deck. My transcripts were their trump. They skirted around every issue and deposited road blocks as they passed. They were determined to keep me sidelined. They were succeeding.

At the time I left Valley Prep, almost everyone knew that I had become serious about my studies. I was feeling good about it and my grade point average even rose to a 2.9, just slightly below a "B" average.

Then my transcripts arrived at the CIF office.

There they were, my official transcripts, signed by Pop Wilson. But the grade point average was 1.9, one-tenth of a point below the required level for academic eligibility. Mysteriously, my average dropped by an entire grade point.

How did they do it? The same way they gave John Pearlman a "B" in Spanish. They changed it. *"We give what we want, we'll take what we want."*

I had been holding my own in the classroom; my teachers could verify that I was passing. But now, here I was, ineligible.

All of my doubts resurfaced. Valley Prep had battered me every step of the way. They could sense the kill, and I could too. My back was to the wall.

I kept it there.

Commissioner Thomas stepped in. The principal from Mater Dei was right behind him, requesting transcripts from Wharton and Central High School, to check my history as a student-athlete. They couldn't make any decisions until they had recovered these transcripts.

Sweating it out—with two schools, a powerful governing body, and a mess of illegalities standing between us and the football field, Preston and I sat and waited. Meanwhile, we performed the same tedious activities—reading, studying, keeping in shape—for what seemed like an eternity.

Finally, after the commission digested all of the information, they called us back to the CIF office and released a statement. "By review, Derek and Preston's grades are greater than a 2.0."

Preston and I sat before the CIF Southern Section Executive Committee, listening, as Mr. Thomas relayed the news with a warm smile. I wanted to spring out of my chair, grab Preston and scream for joy, but I was too busy breathing again. I felt like my life was given back to me.

Preston felt the same. We sank deep into our chairs, shook our heads at each other and just giggled.

Mater Dei's principal stood up and spoke about his disappointment at the media for saying that our grade point averages were below the required 2.0.

Addressing the commission, he said, "If somehow I can tell you without having it distorted in the media, as the principal at Mater Dei, Derek Sparks is a "B" student.

"When I reviewed his transcripts I saw a kid who could go on to Notre Dame or any Ivy League school. He might need some tutoring in some areas, but with his talents he is the type of kid we want to attend Mater Dei High School."

Those were just the words I needed to hear. The rest, we could sort out later. I had arrived!

Now it was time to settle matters on the field. The city could judge whether I was worth the effort.

The Mater Dei Monarchs were scheduled to play at home on Friday night against Santa Ana. On the depth chart, for the first time, in what seemed like months, I read *"Starting tailback, No. 5, Derek Sparks."*

(from left) Father Weding, Principal
Pat Murphy and former Principal Lyle Porter
welcome Moms and me to Mater Dei.

38. SHOWTIME

Who am I kidding? I was nervous, I just didn't want to admit it to myself. It was time to put up or shut up.

The pressure had been building for a long time, and something had to give. Every day for the past few months, my name was somewhere in the local sports pages. This had happened a lot during my life, but now the press was negative.

**MATER DEI HAS
IMAGE PROBLEM**

The private school has been criticized for enrolling transfers Derek and Preston Sparks.

I wasn't used to this. I was seeing my name constantly linked with the word "controversial" or "problem."

The controversy led to speculation. Can Derek run the football? Is he a student or just a jock? Was Derek Sparks worth all the trouble? On and on.

MARK BOSTER / Los Angeles Times
Mater Dei High School is trying to restore its image after enrolling Derek, (left), and Preston sparks.

On any given day there was at least one newspaper column devoted to my inability to compete at a big school, my inflated numbers or my "rightful place" at a small school back in the Valley.

Still, I believed in myself. I had made some bad decisions but that was over. I knew where I was headed and how to get there. There would be no more illegalities. Everything I did would be accomplished in the broad daylight and by the rules.

Since leaving Valley Prep, the phone calls from colleges had nearly stopped. I knew that I had to make some noise on the field. I had to let them know the obituaries were false. I was alive and, although I was no longer number one, I was still one of the top running backs in the country.

I only wished that I didn't have to prove it after two weeks of inactivity. Joining a new offense with a new group of guys was my biggest worry. All day long, through school and practice, I kept telling myself, "You're not nervous, D. You can do it. You're not nervous."

It wasn't helping.

I was pushing too hard in practice to be ready and aggravated an already weak ankle that I had injured in the Hawaii game. An ankle injury is one of those nagging impairments that only heals with rest and time.

Time was the one thing I didn't have, with my first game coming in a matter of days. I had to play. I spent hours every day getting physical therapy, hoping the ankle would hold out for me.

Game day arrived and I entered the stadium a mess. I felt completely outside of myself. My head and body were nothing more than a convoluted ball of anxiety.

I sat in the locker room, put my headphones on and asked BeBe and CeCe to grant me some clarity. Something holy.

I never pray to win. That night I simply prayed that God would give me the strength to deal with the pressure to perform. To perform to best of my ability, and to help me leave every inch of myself out on that field.

The music blasted its way inside of me. *"Hold up the light!"* I had jammed to this tape a hundred times before, but the words were giving me a whole new meaning. *"Hold up the light...Save the world from darkness..."*

God had given me talents, and now it was time to use them.

Showtime!

Friday night, and the stadium was ablaze in lights. I felt nearly overwhelmed. There must have been fifteen thousand people in the stands, all of them yelling and screaming. When we hit the field, I could hear a noise building from the crowd. Thousands of people grumbling something in unison.

The grumbling became clear. Soon, they began to shout it, "SPARKS...SPARKS...SPARKS..." Fifteen thousand people, coming to see me play, to see if I was for real. For the first time in my life I felt butterflies on a football field.

I tried to tune the crowd out, but there was no chance of that on this night. As they chanted my name the noise was overpowering. I was afraid to look into the stands, but for some reason, I felt compelled. And I was glad I did. It was the first time since Wharton that I looked into the stands and saw my mother.

There she was, sitting up there cheering me on. She smiled as if to say "Can you believe this?" She blew me a kiss and joined the chants. "SPARKS...SPARKS...SPARKS..." I looked at her one more time before turning towards the field.

I glanced over to the sidelines. There was Preston. He was wearing my practice jersey. We had always done things like this to show our love and support for each other, but this was getting to be too much for me. I was choked with emotion. I needed to get the game going, even if it meant that I would play terribly. Let's just get this thing going.

The players from the Los Angeles Rams kept their promise and came back. Some of the players called to me from the far end of the Mater Dei bench.

"Hey, Showtime, are you ready to shake it up?"

I didn't answer. These guys were calling me *Showtime!* I just nodded and kept my game face on. How could anybody be ready for all of this?

We lost the toss. Santa Ana chose to receive, and in doing so, prolonged my agony. So I did what I had done the week before, I waited anxiously on the sidelines. This time, though, I was in a Monarch uniform standing next to Coach Rollinson.

I was terrified that the cellular phone would ring; some CIF official sounding voice telling me I couldn't play. Maybe one of the coaches from Valley Prep would be on the line, laughing to the bitter end, with one last trick up his sleeve. I tried to clear my mind.

The defense set the tempo early, forcing Santa Ana to punt. The crowd roared. I looked at Coach Rollinson. He winked at me and said, "Big D, take us to the Promise Land."

I winked back and ran onto the field with the offense.

In the huddle, Billy Blanton was taking charge.

"I guess we all know the first play is going to Derek."

It was. The coach sent in a "16 Zone." That's a play where I would run off tackle and try to grind out a quick five or six yards.

Before we broke the huddle, one of the linemen spoke up.

"Hey, we know how important this game is. I'm gonna open up a nice big hole for you, D. Do what you do best."

My heart was racing, adrenaline pumping. I nodded and flashed them the victory sign.

I could hardly hear the cadence. The noise was deafening. I took a glance at the defense and zeroed in on the quarterback. Blanton got the snap and spun in my direction. I took the hand-off cleanly.

As I charged by, Blanton screamed at me. "Go!"

That lineman hadn't lied. He opened up a good-sized hole and I hit it like a steam engine.

Wharton, Central, Valley Prep, Mater Dei...same field, same moves.

Everything was clear again. I gave the linebacker a shoulder move. I cut hard to the outside. I thought about my ankle for a second but decided to pour it on anyway. Now or never.

The cut bought me an extra step. I dug my cleats deep into the grass, accelerated, and made the cut up field towards the sideline. I poured on the speed while the defenders were still trying to adjust. Too late. I flew down the sideline untouched and never stopped. It was an 80 yard touchdown!

The crowd went wild. I let the ball drop and roll, as I had done so many times before, but this was different. I was back! I scored on my first carry as a Monarch. Wait! It wasn't just a score, it was an explosion!

Preston was on the sideline, screaming at me near the end zone. After I dropped to one knee and gave thanks, I ran straight to him and gave him a high five.

I found the lineman who opened the hole and thanked him. He looked at me with a weird expression. All he could say was, "Wow."

I was just getting started. My second 80 yard touchdown came on my second carry. Now I could hear the crowd loud and clear.

"SPARKS...SPARKS...SPARKS...!"

I looked up, pointed to the sky, and, even though I had little breath in me, I yelled, "Thank you, Jesus!" The stadium noise was so loud no one could hear me. I knew He could.

I found the left side tackle and ran arm-in-arm back to the sideline. I wanted him to share in the moment. He was jazzed.

The Los Angeles Rams players on the sideline hollered, "Showti-i-i-ime!"

I tried to find my mom in the stands, but it was all too crazy. I found Preston and stayed with him. I wanted to be with someone I trusted, who would keep my head in the game.

On our third possession, from the 38-yard line, the call came in, "16 Zone." The fullback, a guy named Scott McKelvey, was standing next to me. He spoke up.

"What a surprise!"

I looked at him, suspecting what he was feeling. Before I came to Mater Dei, he had been the workhorse of the team, the guy you counted on to ground out the yards and score touchdowns. Now he might be feeling like an extra in the Derek Sparks Show.

When our eyes met, I saw that he had no animosity. He looked at me intently and said, "Let's get it done."

That was his way of saying he'd do whatever it took to win. We broke the huddle and Blanton took the snap. As he stuck the football in my gut I saw a hole emerge between two of our linemen. My adrenaline pushed me through the hole while my eyes stayed focused on the end zone.

Three carries. Three touchdowns.

"SPARKS...SPARKS...SPARKS...!"

I was really back!

We left the field at the half leading 21-6. I had gained 229 yards on 3 carries.

The final score was 38-21, Mater Dei's first win of the season, and a better comeback than I could have ever imagined. I was overwhelmed. Overwhelmed and thankful.

The week that followed was crazy. Everywhere I went people were talking about the game. I had become a campus celebrity within a week. Even my teachers talked about it during class. Crazy.

In spite of the accolades, I worried the next day as I scooped up all the local papers. The college recruiters had always responded to me according to the newspaper reports, and my future couldn't handle any more dirt.

When I opened the *Orange County Register,* I sighed with relief and smiled. I had been named their High School Player of the Week.

I checked the *Orange Coast Daily Pilot*...Player of the Week.

I groped for another newspaper. The headline flew up at me:

SPARKS BEGETS FIRE, AND THE MONARCHS LIGHT UP OFF DEREK'S STERLING EFFORT

Derek Sparks, whose dream is to carry the football in the NFL, never imagined it this way...

Ygnacio Nanetti/The Orange County Register
Derek Sparks leaves Santa Ana defenders behind as he scores his third touchdown for Mater Dei on Sept. 21.

A record breaking night in my first appearance as a Monarch.

Billy Blanton turned out to be a great quarterback.

I was giggly until I looked at the last unopened paper in front of me. The *Los Angeles Times*, the leading newspaper in the Southland, rested before me, patiently waiting until I was ready to receive its verdict. The paper was crumbling in my hands as I kept curling the corner of the first page, quickly closing it. Finally, I gingerly peeled open the Sports section with one eye half opened.

BOY'S ATHLETE OF THE WEEK

While I was going through all of the newspapers there was a knock at the door. It was Robert Epps, our landlord. He was excited, ranting and raving about my performance. I almost had to laugh, but something told me not to take this guy lightly. He hadn't made all this money being a fool, so I let him do most of the talking.

"Derek, I saw that game you played the other night. That was something. That was really something."

From the beginning, he had been lukewarm on the idea of helping some high school football players. Now his outlook had changed dramatically.

I remained expressionless, listening.

"...I mean, really something," he said. "Are you all comfortable here? Is there anything you need?"

"Not really," I said.

"Hee-hee. Not really? Well, that's good. That's very good. Listen, a guy like you is going to need to get around. We should see about getting you a car. Can't have you sitting on bus stops breathing in all that filth. How about that?"

"I don't really need to get anywhere," I said. "School is just around the corner."

"Derek, I'm not talking about a car, you know, like the ones those kids you go to school with drive. What I mean is a real car. Say, like a brand new BMW?"

He was speaking my language now. A Beemer was my dream car. Man, I could see myself cruising around in a brand new BMW.

"Convertible?"

"Convertible! Why not? No sense driving a luxury car if you don't have all the luxury. Am I right?"

"Right."

"So don't you worry about it. I'll just take care of everything."

Epps had uttered the magic sentence. The alarms went off everywhere in my head. I didn't go through all this garbage just to grab at the first carrot someone dangled in front of me. I thought a BMW would be nice, but I came back to earth in a hurry.

"I'm going to have to discuss this with Jay," I said. "I'll let you know."

This caught him off guard but he recovered quickly.

"Sure, sure, you think about it. Take your time. I'll let you get your rest. You have a good day now. Hey, the other night? That was really something."

"If you think that's something, you should see Preston play," I said.

"Oh, my!" he said with excitement. He went on and on as he nearly skipped down the front walk. I had to laugh.

Meanwhile, at the CIF Southern Section office, Stan Thomas was not happy about our allegations regarding Valley Prep. He wasn't about to drop the ball and allow the school to continue as it had.

He declared Preston ineligible. Preston's transcripts indicated that he hadn't completed the necessary units. The delay of his transcripts and the discrepancy between his earned GPA and those noted was a big problem. Commissioner Thomas smelled a rat, and he didn't like rats running schools for kids.

The only question was how he would deal with the illegal activities discovered at Valley Prep. What sanction could he pass to prevent this same situation from occurring to student-athletes in the future?

Thomas called the Valley Prep administration to the table. He asked them to double check their records. If Preston had not completed the units necessary to be eligible, Valley Prep must deliver an explanation as to why they had allowed this teenager to participate in football, basketball and baseball. He would clearly have been ineligible, which meant an immediate forfeiture of Valley Prep's baseball championship.

Serious penalties existed for schools allowing ineligible players to compete on athletic teams and Thomas communicated this threat clearly.

His voice was low and precise as he suggested that Valley Prep scrutinize their records and verify their paperwork.

What do you know, a new transcript appeared. On this official document it showed that Preston had completed more classes than the original transcripts had indicated. It was hilarious.

The classes were Computer Science and Spanish. Can you imagine a conversation in Spanish between Preston and John Pearlman? Well maybe you can't. But trust me, it sounded a lot like English.

Valley Prep was snagged in their own trap. They had fixed up classes for athletes and then tried to withhold the credits to prevent us from transferring to Mater Dei. Thomas busted them.

Suddenly, the commission announced that Preston would be eligible to play football for Mater Dei. We couldn't believe it! Preston and I exploded with joy, jumping around the house like two little kids.

It was the most happiness our home had experienced in a long time. I had been hurting over Preston's situation, and now a big weight had been lifted off me. What a relief, the dream was alive again. Really alive!

Thomas was no pushover though. He mandated Preston not to play a down of football until it was clear that he could handle the curriculum at Mater Dei. He wasn't allowing Preston to play in Friday's game. He would have to get his head seriously into his books to prove that he meant business.

When I talked with Jay, I suggested that we get a tutor to help us maintain in the classroom.

"Wake up, D," said Jay. "Do you really think anybody at Mater Dei is going to keep you guys off the field? The way you run and the way Preston catches? Open your eyes, D."

Jay's remarks caught me off guard. I wondered why Jay was even telling me this, when Mater Dei had been nothing but good to us. I shrugged and tucked the thought away. I had my second game against Riverside to think about.

I still had a lot to prove and many critics to silence. The word was going around that Santa Ana was a pushover, and that I hadn't really been tested. The word was that against a bruising defense like Riverside, I would fold.

They were right about Riverside's defense. These guys were hard hitters who didn't go for fancy moves. And there was no easy yardage in that game. I slashed, burrowed and bruised my way to 197 yards on 27 carries. We went on to win the game 31-7.

After that game nobody could say I wasn't a tough, hard-nosed runner. I had grounded out 197 yards, not by being fancy, but by running right at them and powering my way forward, just like my boyhood hero, Tony Dorsett.

It was a good victory, elevating our record to two and two. For the second consecutive week my name appeared in the newspapers, the *Orange County Register* reported.

But what was next? Does God watch you and wait for you to breathe a sigh of relief before hitting you with the next challenge?

Meter Del's Derek Sparks (5) raises his hand in a symbolic gesture during the singing of the alma mater before the Riverside Poly game.

EYE OF THE STORM
Controversy has followed Derek Sparks on his 4 prep stops in 4 years.

When I picked up the phone that evening, the pattern felt like a bad joke.

"Hey traitor."

It was Coach Hutchinson. I knew better than to say anything.

"What did we ever do to you to make you treat us so bad? Man, your uncles are a big pain in the butt. They're making our lives pretty miserable over here, all because they can't keep their mouths shut. And you? You're not helping.

"Well, I got news for you," he said, giving me no opportunity to say anything, even if I wanted to. "I talked to Terry Donahue, and you can scratch UCLA off your list, because I told them what a pain in the butt you and your whole family are. They wouldn't give you a scholarship if you if you were the last two-legged football player in the city. How do you like that? Huh?

"Don't say I didn't warn you. You should'a been loyal to the program. Everything we did, we did for you. You got a lot of talent, but you're so damn stupid I can't even believe it. You had it all, and now I'm gonna make it my personal business to see that you get nothing."

Again he hung up before I could say a word.

I reacted differently to this call than I had to earlier ones. Hearing the hate in Coach Hutchinson's voice, as he threatened to ruin my future, I realized that his whole life had become a series of distortions and rationalizations. He had probably even convinced himself that all of his actions were for my benefit.

That bothered me more than anything. Adults in charge didn't seem to know the difference between right and wrong. They didn't know the difference between guidance and manipulation. For them, the game was about money, fame and moving up at the complete sacrifice of conscience. It was all about winning!

We had always heard, "It's not whether you win or lose..." But it was. It was all about wining. And to win, to be sure you'd win, you had to play the game their way.

I couldn't rebound from Hutchinson's words, and it showed in our game against Mission. I was completely distracted and I don't remember much about the game. Only that we lost 42-23, and I only gained 125 yards.

It hurt even more because it was Preston's debut. I wanted it to be a sweet memory for him. It wasn't.

That game got the media buzzing again. They picked up where they'd left off, with speculations about my ability or, the lack of it. The calls from reporters began to pour in again, asking if I wanted to return to Valley Prep, if I was beginning to doubt my decision.

I had to work hard not to get angry at these guys. They knew what they were doing. The reporters were trying to lure me into saying something worthy of a scandal. Hey, I had come to the team in the third game of the season. I rushed for 603 yards, was ranked sixth in the CIF Southern Section and I averaged 10.3 yards per carry. I'd had one less than spectacular game, and now they were asking me if I wanted to flee back to Valley Prep? It wasn't right.

It didn't end with me. They were stirring up a lot of trouble for the school too. Although my transfer to Mater Dei was strictly above board, under the watchful eye of Commissioner Thomas, the transfer caused many other schools and the media to scream foul play.

I had no way of knowing that the school had been penalized the year before for the illegal inducement of Danny O'Neil, who went on to become their star quarterback. I knew nothing of this, but it was just my luck to wind up somewhere with an already tainted reputation for recruiting.

The media was having a feeding frenzy.

Mater Dei had been cleared of the charges in the previous scandal. Now, the media couldn't really have a story about the school's questionable recruiting tactics without focusing on me, the "controversial" running back. I couldn't get away from it.

Tension mounted between the school, the media and the CIF Southern Section office. In the end, Commissioner Thomas announced his satisfaction that the school was playing by the book. The furor died down, but for my image and my future the damage had already been done.

All I could do was try to bounce back, play good football and excel in the classroom. That was my only means of defense.

Coach Hutchinson's words remained in my head. How much damage could he really do to me? I was anxious, especially with phone calls from recruiters becoming a distant memory.

"Just run the football, D," I told myself. What else could I do?

So, I did. I put all of my focus on the team and made every effort to pull us closer together.

I respected Coach Rollinson. He was a player's coach, the kind I liked. And it appeared that he liked me as well. He never jumped to conclusions about my past. Not once. Furthermore, he always defended me to the media or to any other hostile critics.

Our next game was against Servite, and I wasn't the only one with something to prove. The whole team was under fire for the way we lost to Mission the week before.

In the locker room the mood was intense before the game. I couldn't help thinking that some of the guys were feeling they would have been better off had I never come to Mater Dei. They were sweating under the hot glare of the spotlight, learning just how vicious the media could be. We needed to stay together.

First and goal.

We were losing 24-14, as the third quarter ticked away the final few seconds.

I lay on the sidelines trying to remember my name. I was in a fog and felt sick to my stomach. I couldn't answer any of the coaches' questions. What was my name? What was my jersey number? Did I know where I was? Every question left me more confused.

The team ran a play. No gain. I swayed on the sideline, not even knowing where I was. Then the coach asked me the one question I was conditioned to answer. "Can you go?"

I said nothing. I just buckled my helmet and teetered onto the field.

The crowd went wild. My stomach churned, as the field spun around and around.

Billy Blanton looked in my eyes in the huddle.

"You all right?"

"Huh?"

"Jesus."

Scott McKelvey said, "Gimme the ball."

"No," I said, almost by instinct. "I got it."

Blanton wasn't sure, but he called the play anyway. We broke the huddle. Blanton pointed for me to stand behind him.

My next memory was of me laying face down in the grass with the goalline inches behind me. The crowd roared in the background as my teammates carried me off the field. We won 28-24.

I just kept looking around, my head hammering. I was trying to figure out how the football got wedged in my arm. Billy stared at me, beaming with pride and happiness, shaking his head in disbelief.

39. DRIVE

The entire season at Mater Dei was an echo of that Servite game. Down one minute, up the next. Breathe, hold it, breathe, hold it...

I hadn't heard a word from any recruiter in weeks, and for the first time in a long while the phone was silent. I had to prove to the colleges that, even with all the controversy, I was still a serious player and a valuable recruit.

I was sure they'd call, so I sat by the phone and waited for it to ring. An activity I don't recommend. There's nothing worse than waiting for something to happen to you.

One evening the phone finally rang. It was a man named Williams with UCLA. He was the recruiting coordinator with whom Preston and I had become friendly during the UCLA camp. Being named the MVP and Runner Up had placed us high on the recruiting list.

"How are you doing, kid?"

"Hanging in there," I said. "What's up?"

"Derek, you're a good kid. Your cousin too..."

I didn't like his tone of voice. I knew that Williams hadn't called to compliment my personality.

"Thanks," I said, already feeling empty.

"If I had my way, you'd be the first two student-athletes we would give full scholarships to..."

I cut him off. "What are you saying, Coach Williams?" I held my breath.

"Kid, you should know what we're hearing over here. The word is, you boys are trouble. They're saying you got these crazy uncles who'll run to the NCAA and scream bloody murder if you guys don't get things done your way.

"But you know I'm not like that," I countered.

"I know it. But Coach Donahue, he doesn't know. And all he hears is that a scholarship for you or Preston is a one year deal and then you're gone. He doesn't want any one year guys."

An even worse thought hit me.

"But you guys were real hot on Preston. He's counting on it," I said.

"Tell him not to," said Williams.

"Is there something I can do? Could I talk to Coach Donahue?"

"It's over, kid. I'm sorry."

Just like that. My chance, Preston's chance, to go to UCLA, was gone. I flew into a rage. I wanted to hurt somebody. Get even.

Then the anger subsided as quickly as it had surfaced. The truth hit me hard and I sat there staring into space for a long while.

It wasn't just Coach Hutchinson who had ruined my chances. It was all of us. We had all become moving parts of the machine. We had played the game, on and off the field, for all of the wrong reasons. We had all tried to win, whether it was for a scholarship or a championship. We tried every way to win except the right way. And the sad thing was, the right way would have been good enough. We all lost.

The game wasn't over though, and no one was going to win by crying or getting angry. The next level of play wasn't going to get any easier either. That much was clear.

Nobody had warned me that the journey would be like this. I wouldn't have believed them had they tried.

Scratch UCLA.

◆◆◆

Game week, Mater Dei v. St. Thomas.

Let's not call it a game; let's call it a circus. St. Thomas officials said some pretty nasty things about Preston and me in the newspapers. They even insulted the way Mater Dei had handled our transfers.

I felt an unusual energy in the locker room before the game against St. Thomas. The whole team wasn't just feeling competitive; they were angry. Coach Rollinson read excerpts from a few of the most recent articles in order to pump the guys into a revenge mode.

During the pre-game activities, evil looks, gestures and tauntings were passed between the teams, from both sides of the line.

Looking back on it, I see that the stage was set for something big to happen. St. Thomas was ranked nationally by *USA Today* and Mater Dei had those talented but troubled Sparks kids.

St. Thomas won the coin toss and elected to kick off to us.

With the football spiraling through the air, I slid under it gracefully. Driven by rage, when the ball landed into my cradled arms, BOOM, I exploded up the right sideline, untouched, 92 yards in a cloud of dust. Touchdown!

The St. Thomas home crowd grew silent.

But wait! There was a penalty flag on the play. One of our players was called for holding. The ball was coming back. No touchdown!

The rest of the game was a defensive dog fight. Neither team gave up an inch. No touchdowns were scored and no big yardage was gained. It was a terrible offensive game. In the end, we upset them 3-0.

Besides the one touchdown they called back, I hadn't spent any time in the end zone. Although we won, the hisses and jeers from the St. Thomas team were almost too much for me to bare.

When the game ended, Tom ran to the center of the field to congratulate me. Right then, the St. Thomas coaches, who were walking out to shake our coach's hand, shouted something at me. It was inaudible, but I knew, by their smirks and grimaces that it was something nasty.

In response, Tom and I did a little victory do-si-do in the middle of the field. I don't know what motivated Uncle Tom, but I felt compelled to rub our victory in their noses.

St. Thomas's head coach went berserk and screamed, "Hey, Sparks, what school are you going to be at *next week*? Not St. Thomas. You'll never be good enough to come to our school!"

Uncle Tom and I kept on dancing.

Their coach yelled to our coach, for all to hear, "You've lost control of your school to a bunch of niggers. That comes from putting athletics first."

Then, he pointed directly at me, in the middle of the field, dancing. "He owns your school!"

I kept dancing. I don't know why though; I wasn't happy.

◆◆◆

The media took the story and ran with it. Everywhere I looked there was a picture of me dancing. Of course the media made me look even more foolish than I felt.

Before I knew it, the newspapers spewed stories and editorials about what a poor sport I was. The timing couldn't have been worse.

I wondered how all of this would affect my standing with colleges. I didn't have to wait long to find out. I got a call from my old backfield mate, Marcus Wright-Fair, who was red shirting at USC.

"D, you messed up this time."

"Oh, you been reading the papers, huh?" I tried to sound casual.

Marcus's tone was serious.

"It's more than that." He went on to fill me in. It turned out that the son of the head coach at USC played quarterback for St. Thomas.

"Coach didn't like what you did, man."

"What *I* did? How did he like what *they* did?"

"It's his son's team, dude. He's pretty pissed off."

Great.

"So, I'm out?"

Marcus didn't skip a beat. "Pretty much."

I had gone, in one year, from visiting the head coach at USC in his private office, to being completely rejected.

Scratch USC.

I had pretty much given up hope of going there even before the incident, since Valley Prep had strong connections with USC. I knew that they wouldn't waste any time in communicating all of their problems with *that Sparks kid*. But bad publicity builds on itself, and clearly I was in trouble.

I called a couple of sportswriters and issued a public apology for my actions following the St. Thomas game. I told the truth. I snapped, I said, after their coach made unfavorable comments about us in the newspapers, leading up to the game, and after he called me a nigger. My emotions got the best of me.

"I got carried away," I said apologetically, "when I heard the awful things they were saying about me."

I don't know if my explanation did anything to ease the tension. At least I tried to set the record straight.

Our playing, meanwhile, was growing lopsided in the loss column. In the next game, against Paramount, we got our butts kicked. You should have seen the headlines.

PARAMOUNT DANCES ALL OVER MATER DEI! (28-11)

I learned my lesson. The message was loud and clear. I would do my dancing on the dance floor, not on the football field.

But no headline phased me like the one I read in the Los Angeles Times:

MATER DEI'S PRESTON SPARKS OUT FOR SEASON

It happens so fast in football. One day you're making the game's winning touchdown; the next day you're injured and facing reconstructive surgery.

I had become comfortable playing with Preston again. But more importantly, I was frightened by what this injury might do to his collegiate hopes. His future was in the air.

Preston never stopped coming to the games. He was hurting, inside and out, but he made sure he was there to cheer me on.

In his honor, I changed my jersey to No. 4.

With Preston injured, watching from the sidelines I played for both of us.

◆◆◆

In our final week of the regular season we defeated St. John Bosco, to move into the Division I playoffs against Long Beach Poly. Nobody had expected us to reach that far.

It made it even sweeter when we blew Long Beach Poly out 58-31. Billy Blanton had a big passing night. I rushed for 222 yards on 22 carries and scored three touchdowns.

Our win over Poly seated us against the number one rated team in the country, Eisenhower.

Victory, 35-20. We had upset the best team in the country! I was even able to put the finishing touches on the win with a 92 yard run. It felt great, but did nothing to ease my anxiety over college. The few college recruiters I had run into since the USC and UCLA rejections, were distant and evasive.

"Yeah, we'll get back to you," was their favorite line.

You watch a guy run for almost 300 yards, score three or four touchdowns, and you'll get back to him? Four years into this journey I was no closer to a scholarship than I had been sitting in the projects in Wharton, Texas.

Our victory over Long Beach Poly

seated us against Eisenhower,

the No. 1 rated team in the country.

40. WAITING

We lost the CIF semi-finals to Quartz Hill, 37-7 in a game that all we did was fumble. I coughed up the ball twice. Billy had three interceptions. We gave them the game. It was terrible.

It wasn't what I'd imagined my last high school game to be, but this wasn't the way I imagined my career unfolding either. Valley Prep had won.

It was time for me to start thinking about playing for a junior college, with the hope of catching on to a university from there. My heart sank every time I envisioned it.

I had a great year by anyone's standards; rushing for 1,704 yards on 240 attempts. I was the *Orange Coast Daily Pilot* Offensive Player of the Year, All CIF Southern Section, and all important, a football All-American.

I was named, along with Napoleon Kaufman, Chris Hayes, Anthony McClanahan, Singor Mobely, Keyshawn Johnson and Lamont Warren to the Best in the West Squad (two points behind Leon Lett who was seriously flirting with USC). I was named to the *L.A. Times* region's best "Terrific Twenty Two."

Only one year before, I'd been pressured into call a press conference to announce that I would *not* forego my senior year of high school to accept an early offer from USC. I had to do it to stop the media speculation that I was going to sign an early letter of intent. But now...

I'd begun the year tabbed as the premier running back in the entire country and I'd delivered the goods. At Mater Dei, we made history, becoming the first team in the school's twenty-four-years to make the semi-final playoffs.

Now I had dropped substantially in the ratings among running backs. I was without a single scholarship offer.

I had a scheduled recruiting visit to a big university in Colorado, the dream of every high school football player. I called two days in advance to confirm, but was told that they had no such trip planned. I got the message. I was unwanted. Valley Prep had to be smiling somewhere in the background.

Colorado, once anxious to recruit me, cooled on the idea after the eruption of so many scandals.

The SAT became my immediate priority. I needed to reach the seven hundred mark, or all of my ambitions were moot. I had scored a miserable five-seventy on my first try. Of course, the second time I scored thirteen hundred points, but we know what that was about.

I knuckled down, becoming intimate with my desktop. I went to the library every day trying to get a handle on the work, but the material was difficult. I had always been a decent student; I just wasn't grasping this.

I made the appointment to take the test, but I didn't tell anyone. I wanted to keep my execution private.

When the day arrived for me to take the SAT again I was almost calm. I had given my preparation a hundred percent. I was glad to enter the testing room feeling so sure of my efforts because when I left, it was without a clue.

I had no idea how I had scored, or if I had even reached the seven hundred mark. That left me with four to six weeks of waiting for my life to arrive in an envelope.

The SAT results had become even more important to me than football. I reasoned that even if I was able to compete in a major university, and go on to the professional ranks, I'd inevitably have to face the real world. It was becoming clear that I needed my degree.

The envelope finally arrived. I kept it in my pocket for a long time. Then I decided to take a walk and open it on the way. I traveled a few blocks from the house before I read the numbers...Six hundred and thirty. Fumble.

I didn't waste any time sulking. I knew what I had to do. I had time to study again, and to retake the test once, maybe twice more before the deadline.

I went to Coach Rollinson and told him I needed to enroll in an SAT prep class. I wasn't cutting it on my own. He wanted to help. He knew the colleges had snubbed me, and he knew I was hurting. He set me up in a class that guaranteed me three hundred points over my previous best score.

I think Coach Rollinson felt sorry for me. He always invited me into his office and asked how I was holding up. How was I getting along? How did I like my classes? Had I had eaten?

I enjoyed our relationship. Coach Rollinson was a good man. He was the first coach who had treated me like a person, not a commodity, meal ticket or stepping stone, as I had been at other schools.

He was a fair coach and he worked in a school that treated me well. I only wished I had discovered Mater Dei sooner. I could only imagine what the results of my career as a student-athlete would have been there.

My life was compressed into Mater Dei studies in the day, SAT studies at night. I was going to pass. I was going to pass. I was going to...

Saturday morning came and I found myself back in the amphitheater among a swarm of faceless students. I thought, "Here I sit—an All-American tailback, with 1,704 yards in one season—scared of two yellow pencils and a blank answer sheet." I had to chuckle.

I looked around the room, wondering how many other students had their futures on the line. Probably all of them. I gave it my best shot.

Then I waited. Again.

The following weeks gave me nothing but time. Time to think about everything. I'd sit on my bed and pull out all the news clippings, the awards, the letters from colleges, all of it. From the eighth grade in Wharton to Mater Dei. I had so much to be proud of and thankful for. Still, I had nothing to show for it.

The phone rang.

"Hello," I said.

"I'd like to speak to Derek Sparks?"

I didn't recognize the voice. "Yeah," I said, "this is Derek."

"Oh Derek. Hello." He paused like it surprised him to be speaking directly to me. "Have you signed a letter of intent with any university yet?"

I tried to figure who was calling and what their angle was. Was it Coach Hutchinson, rubbing it in? Maybe a newspaper reporter, waiting to deliver the final blow?

"Nah," I said almost flippantly.

"Well we'd like the chance to talk to you."

"Who are you? And no games, please," I said.

"This is Mike Price. The head football coach at Washington State University."

"The Huskies?"

"No, the Cougars."

"Talk about what?"

There was a long pause. I figured the other shoe was getting ready to drop. I waited for the payoff to the gag.

"About you playing for the Cougs."

It was for real. Washington State University was interested in offering me a scholarship. I didn't know how to react. I had never considered Washington State before. Before, that is, the stars in my eyes had faded.

Now I couldn't afford to be choosy. It was a Pac-10 school, a great school that had always stood in the shadow of the publicity curtain of the bigger name schools.

Still, I knew better than to get my hopes up. It would only take one negative phone call or a little digging to send these guys scurrying back to *the Palouse,* which is, by the way, one of the most beautiful sections of the Pacific Northwest. But it sure felt good to have somebody step forward, saying that they thought I was worth recruiting.

I guess good news is contagious. A couple of days later I received calls from three schools: the University of Arkansas, Oklahoma, and Miami. Soon, Illinois joined the hunt. This brought me a grand total of five Division I schools in the whole country that wanted to take a chance on this controversial "four-schools-in-four years" kid.

Still I couldn't allow myself to get excited. I couldn't assume anything, from any university, until I held the letter of intent in my hands.

My SAT results arrived first. There was no time for ceremony. I ripped it open right away.

My score was six-ninety, ten points away, with only one chance left to pass.

All five schools were serious, but I only took recruiting trips to three campuses. It was clear they all had the same impression of me. *How could this farm boy be as much trouble as they say he is?*

Every meeting went well, but they all ended on the same note. "We'll need you to send us a passing SAT score before we can sign you."

It had been a long time since I felt ashamed of being Derek Sparks. I laid it on the line about my scores. I told all of the college coaches that I planned to retake the test.

They were all dumbfounded. They regarded my confession as an apparition. "Maybe," I thought to myself, "these coaches were accustomed to dealing with players who had their scores, like their careers, managed for them." It was becoming obvious that I wasn't the only player who had bought the line, *"We'll take care of it."*

Not anymore. I would play at a university because *I* passed the SAT on my own. If I failed, well, I pushed that thought out of my mind. I was going to exert the same energy I put on the football field into passing the SAT. There were no other options.

I wanted no part of all the things that could be taken care of. That was not the type of man I planned to become.

I got to work studying for my fourth try at the SAT, this time without a prep class. I studied like a madman. I hit the books day and night, with no football games or practices to sidetrack me. So this is what it felt like to be a real student?

I knew that my entire future depended on the outcome of this exam, and it made the pressure that much greater. On the morning of the test I felt that I couldn't handle another minute of preparation. My hands were shaking when I broke the seal on the test booklet. My fingers were numb and my hands were clammy as I wrote my name at the top of the answer sheet.

The next three hours were a blur. The following few weeks, waiting for the results, were a lesson in torture. I had nothing to distract me from the reality of my predicament.

Every day one of the schools called me to check in. Had I heard anything? Every day I'd tell them, "Not yet." Reporters called to ask what my plans were. I couldn't say a word, so I just told them the truth. I didn't know.

Jay tried to ask what school I was going to choose. I still hadn't made a final decision, but I definitely had my favorites.

Every conversation with him made me uncomfortable. It felt like he was holding something back. One day I asked what was on his mind. He pulled his chair up close.

"Have you given any thought to Preston's position?" Preston had received offers from only a couple of schools. New Mexico and a smaller school in Idaho. I hadn't become involved because I knew he wanted to drop the "Derek's cousin" from the front of his name.

Jay wanted Preston to go to college with me. He ran down his reasons. The most important was that Uncle Jay didn't want Preston to be on his own.

I got the message. I knew what Jay was asking me to do and frankly it felt right. Preston and I had been together for a long time. If my name could help him get into a better school, that was cool. I wasn't so sure my name was all that strong at the moment, but it wouldn't hurt to ask.

I asked the five schools if they had an interest in recruiting Preston as well. They all said they'd get back to me.

Preston had just taken his SAT for the second time and was waiting for his results. He didn't seem as anxious for himself as I was for him. But between studying and his knee rehabilitation, he kept himself busy.

The schools continued to call every day. They knew the media would follow me wherever I went and they wanted everything neat, clean and above board. If my scores weren't over seven hundred, it would be the last call I'd get from any of them. The pressure made it agonizing to wait for the mail each day. Still no results.

One day I missed getting the mail. Hours passed before I realized that it was sitting on the kitchen table, with my test results in the stack. It didn't seem to matter how I opened it. I had tried waiting, walking, ripping, peeling, it all came out the same. So, I sat on my bed and opened it up.

There it was. Six hundred and ninety. Again.

I was ten points shy. One or two questions on the test stood between me and my dream. Ten points.

I climbed into the shower with all my clothes on, letting the water drown me. I tried to cool the burning inside but there wasn't enough water in all the world to quench the fire. It was the end of the line.

There was no sense prolonging things. I would have to call the schools and give them the bad news. I wanted to thank them personally for believing in me, for giving me a shot, and for seeing past the machine and all of its hype.

The last coach I contacted was Jim Zeches at Washington State University. He was very sympathetic. I'm sure that he realized it was a difficult phone call to make. I thanked him and told him how sorry I was that I hadn't come through. He told me he appreciated my being up front with him.

I was about to hang up when...

"It's a shame," he said. "Now you'll have to sit out your first year here."

I had such a lump in my throat that I couldn't speak.

The deal was still on. They were just planning to "Prop. 48" me until I could raise my SAT scores. Proposition 48 was the NCAA's "no pass, no play" rule that allowed players to attend school at their own expense.

Washington State could monitor my academic progress to make sure I had an opportunity to become eligible. They still wanted me! I ended the conversation politely, hung up the phone and then let out a scream like you've never heard before. I was going to college!

The other four schools responded in exactly the same way. I actually had a decision to make. I couldn't believe that, through all of this, I'd still have an option as to where I wanted to attend school.

I weighed all the factors: the people, the campuses, the conferences they were in and athletes who had played there and had gone on to the pros. In the end, my decision wasn't very scientific. I chose the one school that wanted both me and Preston.

41. DECISION

Washington State University.

This dream seemed to have more lives than a cat. Lucky for me.

I was going to hold a press conference to announce that I had chosen to become a Washington State Cougar in the fall. I'd be an entering freshman, but I would be ineligible to play my first year.

I felt shabby and humiliated to have to tell the world that I couldn't cut it academically. Especially since I knew many guys playing college ball who had their SAT taken for them. Although they'd passed, I knew that they couldn't have scored half of what I had on their own. But *they* were playing the game.

Coach Zeches called me late one night.

"Are you registered to take the SAT tomorrow?" he asked.

"No," I said.

"Take the test again," he said.

"Can't," I said. "There's no time to study."

"Don't study," he said. "Take it. What have you got to lose? I mean, ten points? You spell your name better you'll get ten more points."

Or, I could drop ten points. But he was right. What did I have to lose? Preston and I ran down the next day and took the test again.

The following week we held our press conference in which we told the media that we were awaiting our test scores, which wasn't entirely untrue. We talked about how much we liked the program and the people at Washington State University. Coach Price was the only coach who actually took the time to sit down and talk to us. He knew the whole story, the accusations, and the media's spin and promised to stick by us.

Coach Price said that he believed in us. It was something I needed to hear. That made me proud to announce my decision.

The media did what the media does. Every column, every report contained the word "controversial." Some were kind, others harsh.

WSU GETS STAR RB, BAGGAGE
Sparks Cousins Both Plan to Play at WSU
Their decisions cap controversial high school careers.

◆◆◆

Over the years Mike Price and I became good friends.

Every newspaper article made a reference to WSU as my fifth school in five years. They didn't care if it made me look bad. It was news and it would sell papers.

Right after the announcement, Jay called me for a talk. I had an awful feeling. I waited to hear that the scholarship was off; that someone had turned WSU around. I braced myself for the bad news.

"Look D, you know I have always wanted what's best for you. None of this has been easy. Now we've finally got you signed up to go off to school, just the way I told you.

"Now, I been talking to Bob Epps and he feels like it's time for the three of us to go see an attorney."

"An attorney? For what?"

"Well you know," said Jay, "Bob and I are the ones that got you the shot after the Valley Prep situation. Seems like it would only be fair for you to commit ten percent when you sign a contract with the NFL."

"Bob and I thought we could just get the paperwork out of the way now."

My mind flew out of my body. I sat there like a lifeless husk. I didn't see anything in the room. I didn't hear anything else he said. I completely froze. So this is what it came down to.

In my heart I felt I owed Jay just about everything. I had dreamed about sharing my success in any way I could, but I didn't want it to happen like this.

Epps had gotten to Jay. If a man like Robert Epps could get to Jay, the man I looked up to as a father, then nothing was sacred. They expected me to sign away a piece of myself so that Epps could feel that his investment was safe, so Jay could finally cash in his marker.

I scrutinized Jay from what seemed like a mile away. I understood where he was coming from. He wanted insurance. Understanding his position hurt me, but I understood.

I was Derek Sparks—a commodity, a kid bought and sold; a kid who was the meal ticket for everyone—family, coaches and investors, since I was 12-years-old.

Sparks flies!

I was the controversial, troubled running back who attended five schools in five years. No guarantees. It was good business to ensure that the investment was safe. Buy your piece before the kid flies away, before the high school machine bows to its college superiors and to a new set of players in a new game.

I wasn't angry at Jay. I was sad. If I accomplished my dream, a line would form to cash in. If I failed, the line would simply scurry behind another kid with a big future.

That conversation would be the cause of a lot of problems within our family, especially between Jay and Tom. When Tom found out that Jay and Robert Epps had contacted an attorney, he confronted his brother. Uncle Tom wanted to know what his cut was going to be.

Many fingers got pointed; a lot of things were said between Jay and Tom that shouldn't have. But, they were all my family and I loved them.

It wasn't until much later that I learned that the money issue drove Uncle Tom back into the arms of Coach Hutchinson and Valley Prep. In short order he would turn against the whole family in order to get paid.

I tried to stay out of everyone's mess and I never spoke to anyone about that ten percent thing. I didn't talk to my uncles, Jay and Tom, to Moms, or Preston. I never mentioned it again. But I never forgot it either.

42. THE PATH

I walk to the mailbox, angry. I am praying not to be so angry.

Everybody is here, just hangin' around to see what I'm going to do next.

With my eyes closed, I see Dante Dickerson. He doesn't speak. He just wipes his nose on his sleeve.

I see Omar. His eyes are glassier than ever. He pulls at my shirt and whispers, "See you in the NFL."

I see Tanya. Jay pushes her away.

Robert Epps nods, dangling keys to a new BMW in one hand and a legal document in the other.

I see John Pearlman, holding his shoulder, crippled by steroids and cortisone shots, down to 95-pounds. He's lying in a hospital bed as doctors attend to him.

I see Tom doing his victory dance. He's high-fiving Pop Wilson and slapping Hutchinson on the back at the same time. He looks back at me with a sick grin. "Blood is thicker than water, D. But it ain't as thick as money."

I see Preston, red-eyed and crying, holding his jersey in one hand, and two papers—his SAT scores and a telegram from the CIF Southern Section—in the other. "Play for me, D," he says.

I see the Valley Prep coaching staff convened around a young starry-eyed football prospect and his eager parents. They are promising him the world.

"Just run the football. Everything else will be taken care of."
And there's that damn letter poking out of the mailbox.

I stare at it for a while.

There's my father. He fits in well with the silence.

Everyone else disappears. It's just my father and me, with not much to say.

I look at him for a long time. I see everything in him except my future.

I look up, my eyes squinting against the sun. He's gone. I'm holding the envelope. I breathe deeply, close my eyes and rip it open.

The sound is jarring, but no louder than the laughter that follows.

I am awake now. It's just the world and me; and the world is bright. It's so very, very bright.

I scored 890 on my SAT. I PASSED!

Graduation day at Mater Dei was a
proud moment for Preston (left), our mothers and me.
I graduated with honors, and a 3.0 GPA.

43. FIRST-AND-TEN

There's a sound, smell, and feel to every football game I ever played. Every game has its own image, its own sensation that makes it special.

This game was *very* special.

I slipped on the crimson and gray uniform for the first time and ran my fingers over the lettering. Washington...State...University. Not even BeBe and CeCe could keep me calm. Not this time.

The rest of the team buzzed around and past me; all of us preparing for the first game. This was our whole reason for being. All of the players were pumped beyond belief to take our home field, hear our crowd and soak in every ounce of excitement. We were ready and willing to feed on that excitement all the way into the opening kickoff.

Out of the corner of my eye I caught a shadow. Someone from the outside had opened the door. I saw the man's image. He silently stepped into the Cougar locker room and looked around in wonderment. The ceremony and decoration of this major university had left him in awe.

The man's eyes took in every inch of the locker room. From the Cougar head stitched into the carpet, the coach's play-board, to the nameplates on the door of every locker holding the immaculate helmets, jerseys and cleats, before settling, at last, on me.

He paused for a minute. He fidgeted with his hands before resigning to hang them at his sides, trying his best to look me in the eyes. He stood at the doorway for a long time.

A couple of teammates stared at him with annoyed expressions, but most continued with their pre-game rituals. One of the assistant coaches stormed in the man's direction, wondering how he had escaped security.

The man looked up at the coach, more timid than ever. He opened his mouth to speak but no words came out.

"Hey guy," said the coach, "you can't come in here."

"Excuse me," I said, stepping forward, brushing some of the players aside and grinning from ear to ear. "He's here to see me."

Jay still didn't say anything. He just returned my hug. I held him for a minute and felt his grip grow tighter. He choked out a few words in a rough whisper.

"Hey there, D."

"Did you get the tickets, Jay?"

He nodded and patted his coat pocket, smiling, blinking back tears. It had been awhile.

I turned around to my coaches and teammates. They looked like an army now, anxious and irritated with our quiet reunion.

"Hey, guys, this is my uncle, Jay. All the way from California." A couple of players waved. One coach gave a curt nod. Jay smiled and the locker room resumed its chaos.

"I'll see you out there Jay, huh?"

He looked me up and down with a silent grin. For the first time in my life Jay seemed much smaller than me. He tapped me on my shoulder pads and walked out.

By now the energy level in the locker room was frenzied, and we were working hard to keep it there. Coach Price was shouting something inspirational, anything, so long as it was loud. We banged helmets, slammed shoulder pads, and screamed at each other until the entire room melted into a huge sonic fortress.

I remember every moment of that game, especially how we charged through the tunnel. We fed on the enthusiasm of our home crowd, watching their numbers grow as the clock approached the opening kickoff.

I remember Coach Price, waving for me to get in the game. Every fiber in me ignited. I sprinted from the sideline, into the huddle, as I entered my first Pac-10 contest as a true freshman, on the command my coach had given almost as an afterthought.

I lined up in the backfield like I had so many times before. At Wharton, Central, Valley Prep, Mater Dei, and now, finally, at Washington State University. The backfield was the one thing that never changed, and never left me.

And then, there was that one person, the only other man who believed that I would go all the way.

I remembered that Jay was taking his seat in the stands. I took a quick glimpse and he looked bigger than a few moments earlier. His timidity disappeared and his smile spread from ear to ear. I caught his eyes and he grew another ten feet. He waved his game program triumphantly to me, to the cameras, to the people next to him, to anyone in the world willing to acknowledge this moment. For Jay, it was just as much his moment as it was mine.

I remember. I flashed my victory sign, took the hand-off, and blasted up field.

First-and-ten.

Uncle Jay, we made it!

First-and-ten, I receive the football from Drew Bledsoe, now quarterback for the New England Patriots.

COUGAR PRIDE

Rushing from the tunnel with the rest of the team, I finally felt like I was in charge of the game I was playing.

Running the football wasn't the only way I could become successful in the game of life. My goal-line was the diploma waiting for me at the end of my four years at WSU.

The biggest run of my life came on graduation day at WSU. I became the first Sparks to graduate from College.

WASHINGTON STATE UNIVERSITY
College of Liberal Arts
The 100th Commencement 1996

WHERE ARE THEY NOW?

THE SPARKS FAMILY

Derek Sparks - In case you are wondering, Washington State University became Derek's final school. He distinguished himself on the gridiron, helping WSU earn slots in the Copper and the Alamo Bowls. Still, every newspaper editorial, interview, and story written about the talented student-athlete, referred to him in one way or another as "Mr. Controversy."

Derek was slowed by his first major football injury during his sophomore year. It required intense rehabilitation and kept him sidelined for that entire season. Having been scared by earlier scandals and injuries, he was not drafted by the NFL, as were many of his former teammates mentioned in this book. Nonetheless, Derek never lost his gridiron dreams and is, today, a free agent with the NFL. In 1998 he was invited to the San Francisco 49ers preseason football camp.

In 1996, Derek Sparks became the first member of his family to receive his college degree, a Bachelor of Arts in Social Sciences, with a minor in Business. [Incidentally, his father, who had never attended any of his son's football games, proudly attended Derek's graduation.] Derek put his degree (and his expertise) to good use in founding a successful marketing company, coaching at a community college and touring the country, speaking to youth and parent groups on what it takes to become a champion in the Game of Life.

Preston Sparks - Failing to pass his SAT, Preston wasn't able to attend Washington State University with his cousin, Derek; but instead, returned to Texas for a year. Receiving a passing grade, he resumed his distinguished football career as a student-athlete at WSU, until he re-injured his knee, which required more surgery and rehabilitation. After one extremely promising year as a Cougar, Preston left WSU, citing irreconcilable differences with his position coach. The university subsequently revoked his scholarship.

For two years, Preston, feeling overwhelmed by circumstances, and depressed over his turbulent past, turned to drugs and alcohol to ease his pain. With treatment and a change of heart, Preston was able to get back on track at Central Washington University, where he excelled both as a student and as an athlete.

With only a few units to complete, Preston Sparks will soon become the second college graduate in his family, with a Communications degree from Central Washington University. Based on his successful college football career, Preston is currently being considered for recruitment by several NFL teams.

Jay Sparks - Uncle Jay and his wife, Gretta, didn't miss any of Derek's games while he played at WSU. They still live in Inglewood and Jay still runs his carpet cleaning business. The Texas Connection never materialized. Jay has not spoken to his brother, Tom, since his testimony reversal at the CIF office. He is still bitter.

Tom Sparks - Fearing he'd lost his "meal ticket." Uncle Tom betrayed his family by recanting his testimony before the CIF Southern Section Executive Committee. At the urgings of administrators at Valley Prep who feared expulsion and heavy fines for their numerous violations, Tom became their defense. Tom was promised money and favors for his reversal, which he received. With that, he incurred the alienation of his brother and many members of the Sparks tight-knit clan. Today he is married, with one son and works for the government somewhere in California.

June Sparks - Stayed in Orange County and worked for a few months, following her son's acceptance to WSU. Upon her return to Texas, where she currently resides, June was able to give her son an envelope containing most of her hard-earned money, to give him a better start than she had had. June continues to be her son's number one fan.

THE MATER DEI DAYS

Mater Dei Catholic High School - Is still dominating in basketball, which is now only second to its outstanding football program. The school has garnered five state championships since 1991, under the leadership of Coach Rollinson.

Coach Bruce Rollinson - Has earned his place as one of the most successful coaches in all of high school football and is still the head football coach at Mater Dei.

Billy Blanton - The Mater Dei Quarterback lead the Monarchs to the CIF Championship the year following Derek's graduation. When last heard from, he had signed with San Diego State University on a full athletic scholarship.

Robert 'Bob' Epps - The friendship with Jay and the Orange County businessman cooled after Derek Sparks went off to WSU. Derek never signed his proposed ten percent contract. Epps passed away a few years later.

THE VALLEY PREP DAYS

John Pearlman - Valley Prep's negligence with John's shoulder injury caused him to have major surgery. His playing days were over with six games into in his senior...or should we say, his fifth year. After all the steroids and pain killers, John wasn't even considered as a college prospect. With an inadequate education and a sixth grade reading level, John still graduated from Valley Prep with flying colors. However, John took his love of risk and people to build a successful business career. He is a devoted Christian and is now in his first year of theology school.

Marcus Wright-Fair - After being picked for the Parade All-American Team, he was offered the fullback position at USC as a "true freshman." Marcus had some problems with the knee he had injured while at Valley Prep. The steroids and cortisone shots before games caught up with him. While at USC, he was charged with rape and subsequently transferred to a smaller school. In order to get his career back on track, he had to undergo major knee surgery. After recovering, Marcus now plays Arena football and is coaching at Valley Prep in the off-season.

Leon Lett - Persuaded by Marcus to sign a letter of intent to USC, Leon never devoted time to his studies. He later lost his scholarship. He was last seen attending a small community college in Nebraska.

Pop Wilson - The founder of Valley Prep is still the school's principal. Since the Sparks case and other lesser scandals kept the school under the microscope, he fired Coach Hutchinson. In subsequent interviews, Pop Wilson has stated repeatedly that the school is trying to stay within the guidelines of the CIF rule book.

Coach Hutchinson - After the Sparks' case, Hutchinson continued to coach at Valley Prep. When another scandal erupted at the school, however, Hutchinson was fired. He is still coaching high school football, somewhere in California.

Coach Santini - A grandson of one of the richest financiers in California, Santini is still the head coach at Valley Prep.

Valley Prep - After signing a written confession of rules violations, Valley Prep was sanctioned by the CIF, kicked out of the league indefinitely and placed on probation for three years. Upon appeal, however, with the recanted testimony of Tom Sparks, Valley Prep was able to negotiate a lesser sentence, resuming both its athletic programs and its questionable practices.

CIF Southern Section - Caught in the middle of the Sparks-Valley Prep controversy, the commission initially barred Valley Prep from post-season play in all sports for one year. They were kicked out of the WAC League indefinitely and barred from football playoffs for two years.

Threatened by Valley Prep with a lawsuit, the CIF Southern Section granted the school's officials an appeals hearing, at which, a chief witness, Tom Sparks, recanted his earlier testimony. As a result, the CIF reduced the penalties it had levied against Valley Prep. The outcome of the appeals hearing were never made public. After receiving death threats, Commissioner Stan Thomas later resigned from office.

Using the Sparks case as its benchmark, the CIF has changed its rules regarding student-athlete transfers.

THE CENTRAL HIGH DAYS

Central High School - After Derek left the Long Beach school, it was business as usual. Eight players, including "Purple Lips," passed their SATs and received scholarships to several Division I universities. The school is still a powerhouse in Southern California high school football.

Keith Walker - After excusing himself from the Central football team, he never received a scholarship and never played football again. Embraced by his extended Crip family, Keith went on to pursue a life of crime and disappeared into the streets of South Central.

Bobby Winfield - Graduated from Central and signed his letter of intent to Stanford. Today he is one of the highest paid and most decorated offensive linemen in the NFL.

'Purple Lips'- Graduated from Central and went on to play football for a university in Arizona. He is now playing football overseas.

Tanya - After leaving Central High School, Tanya and Derek kept in contact until he was a sophomore at WSU. They haven't spoken since. But, says Derek, when he closes his eyes, he can still see her smile when she flashes the "victory sign."

THE WHARTON, TEXAS DAYS

Omar Marks - He continued to pursue his dream of earning a college scholarship and moving into a professional career in football. Although he never played on the same collegiate field against Derek, he attended a small college in Kansas and enjoyed a short-lived career on the gridiron. Flunking out of school, Omar returned to Wharton and is now serving a lengthy prison sentence for selling crack cocaine.

Dante "Buckwheat" Dickerson - After a decent career at nearby Boling High School, Dante went on to play football at a small college out of state. He now lives in Wharton with his girlfriend and their daughter.

Wharton, Texas - Is even poorer than when Derek was living there. Drugs, alcohol, homicide and the state penitentiary are the major industries in this dusty, depressing southwest Texas town. Derek's family members are still there, still poor, and still just getting by.

AFTERWORD

BY Pastor Maxie F. James

"For God so loved the world that He gave His only Son, so that everyone who believes in Him may not perish but have eternal life."

The ministry of God is to the world, for the sake of the world. And it is in the world that the continuing ministry of Christ is carried out by the people of God.

Now, here, we find this young man, Derek Sparks, living as a survivor of poor choices made by the people that were in charge of his young life, and himself. The difference is that as Derek moved into a clear knowledge and understanding of his destiny.

Destiny alone raised questions for Derek as to why his particular trials, tribulations, heartache, and pain should visit him at such an early age. These unanswered questions caused Derek to look for understanding as Truth.

Truth is a hard thing to find in a world that tries hard to hide it. The search for truth led Derek on a long spiritual adventure. The truth was God, and God was the revelation that seized him.

God and Truth came together within Derek with a vengeance, destroying his disbelief and taking hold of his destiny.

Moreover, Derek experienced a power that caused everything to work out for his good; turning a victim into a vessel in the mist of pain.

As Derek began to learn his Lessons of the Game, he found out that there is but one lesson to learn. *"Seek ye first the Kingdom of God and His righteousness, and all these things will be added unto you."*

Seeking the Kingdom of God is in direct conflict with the world. But the worldly standards cannot measure the task of a Christian. Only God has the ability to adequately measure a Christian.

When I think of Derek, I think of all who ask, "Where has my struggle led me?" Derek's book on his life calls young people, old people and all people to trust in the love of God and to believe in the power that destiny plays in the outcome of all lives.

Derek returns to us, not as a victim, but as a humbled and well-informed Prodigal Son, sharing all of the outrage, victory and passion which God has visited upon his young life.

ACKNOWLEDGEMENTS

First, giving honor and glory to God, my father, who is truly the head of my life. Thank you, Jesus, for shedding Your blood so that I might have life, and for giving me the strength and wisdom to weather this storm. Even through the most trying circumstances and darkest times You showed Yourself and Your Word faithful. Thank you for my Pastor, Maxie F. James, whom You used to bring forth clarity in my life. It was the strength and love placed in him that made me understand that I will forever serve You and witness to others that You are my provider, shield, comforter, deliverer, and healer. Thank You for all that I have endured and for allowing me to share these experiences with others.

I know that this book is not the result of my strength or of my might; but it is by Your Spirit that it was completed. It is through You that all things are possible. It delights me to say that You are Kings of Kings, Lord of Lords and the one and only GOD Almighty! I shout for joy, because "AIN'T NOBODY BAD LIKE JESUS! NOT EVEN CLOSE!"

SPECIAL THANKS
Jessica, Pam & Bob Burkland.

THE TEAM
Katrina Kumbera, Stuart Robinson, Thomas Black, John "J.T." Wiegman, Stephen Emerick, Valerie Shaw, Dotti Albertine, Susan Nickells, Eric Mai, Mary & Mike Clift, Jenny Morgan, Arianne Simpson, PSM, Milton C. Grimes.

ACKNOWLEDGEMENTS

EXTENDED THANKS
Jaelyn & Nicole Harrison, Leland Sparks, The Sparks Family, Charlene
Calhoun, Tanya-Hannah and the Osborne Family, Katie-Maine-Kesha-
Cedric-Brenda, Erin-Jill-Don Eisner, Bennie Harris, Phi Beta Sigma Bros.,
WSU, Mater Dei High School, Bruce Rollinson, Lyle Porter, Anne M.
Dowden, Bruce A. Dybens, Timothy Esser, Sharon Closson, Kirston
Obergh, George "IKE" Bates, Dr. Shields, Robert Olie, Tom Metzger,
Stephen Baksay, Brendan M. Murray, Glen Armstrong, Kenneth E. Gibson,
Lynn Davis, Guy Thomas, Mike Petrizzo, Chris Repurto, Mike Corroll,
Linda Mittelhammer, Jeoffrey, John Hopkins, Jenny O' Callahan, Walter
Little, Denton and the Calhoun Family.

FIELD OF BROKEN DREAMS (RIP)
Kevin Copland, Deoland Martin, Stanley Calhoun, Carl Maxey, Homer
Saunders, Hank Gathers, Kriston Palomo, Adrian Taufaasau, Donnie
Moore, Eric Hoggatt, Craig Kelford, Heath Taylor, Len Bias.

REFERENCES

Although the names of a few participants have been changed in some excerpts, all newspaper articles actually appeared in the following publications:

The Daily Breeze
The Long Beach Press-Telegram
The Los Angeles Herald Examiner
The Los Angeles Times
The Orange County Daily Pilot
The Orange County Register

Photos in Chapter 43 appear courtesy of
Washington State University Sports Information.

To book your school and youth groups for
Derek Sparks' *Lessons of the Game* Motivation Program,
please call: **1-888-461-GAME**
or e-mail: GametimePublishing@msn.Com

*Until then, don't let your circumstances paralyze
your quest towards achieving your dreams.*

D. Sparks